How to integrate comprehension, vocabulary, and writing across the disciplines.

Questions from the Classroom

Karen D. Wood & Lina B. Soares

Association for Middle Level Education

ISBN 978-1-56090-270-6

Library of Congress Cataloging-in-Publication Data

Wood, Karen D.

How to integrate comprehension, vocabulary, and writing across the disciplines : questions from the classroom / Karen D. Wood & Lina B. Soares.

   pages cm

Includes bibliographical references and index.

ISBN 978-1-56090-270-6 (alk. paper)

1. Language arts--Correlation with content subjects. 2. Language arts (Middle school) 3. Middle school education. I. Soares, Lina Bell. II. Title.

LB1631.W588 2015

428.0071'2--dc23

                                2015012553

Association for Middle Level Education
4151 Executive Parkway, Suite 300
Westerville, Ohio 43081 | www.amle.org

Dedication

This book is dedicated to our fellow educators, all of the middle school teachers across the country and the incredible work they do teaching and reaching our nation's adolescent learners. We appreciate you!

Karen D. Wood & Lina B. Soares

Felice N. DeSouza

Preface

As all middle school educators know, the need to integrate literacy across the curriculum is a goal of every discipline and is consistently included in the standards for each professional area. Add to this cross-disciplinary emphasis on incorporating reading and writing throughout our teaching, the Common Core Standards adopted by over 45 states in our country includes a very broad and all-encompassing focus on literacy as well. So that brings us to the purpose of this book.

We originally planned to address this need for an integrative literacy approach to teaching by making the contents of the "Research to Practice" column in the *Middle School Journal*, a mainstay since 1986, readily accessible in one volume. According to former editors (Drs. Lounsbury, Dickinson, and Virtue), the "Research to Practice" column has been one of the most widely read features in the *Middle School Journal*, hence its staying power through the years.

We saw a way to highlight and perhaps simply reprint or abbreviate some of the columns over the past ten years and subsume the contents under three main categories. Comprehension, Vocabulary, and Writing Connections. But, as we worked with editors at AMLE, our original plan took a different turn and we collectively decided to turn these columns into a more traditional book format, hence the new title. **How to Integrate Comprehension, Vocabulary, and Writing across the Disciplines. Questions from the Classroom**. We include at the end of each section, a list of the Research to Practice columns and the co-authors involved in the writing of the columns to acknowledge their expertise and contributions.

While this book will provide readers with a research and theoretical base, most significantly, it will provide practical strategies for integrating the communication processes across the curriculum. Step- by- step procedures and sample lessons are provided that address all of the subject areas: mathematics, science, social studies, language arts, etc. Each of the three major sections will begin with a brief review of the current research and an overview of the contents to follow.

This book is intended for middle level teachers in all disciplines. It is also a must-read for administrators, curriculum coordinators, assistant principals, literacy specialists, and any other individuals involved in instruction in the middle school.

Both authors, Karen Wood and Lina Soares, are former middle school teachers who understand the questions from the classroom.

So, we hope you enjoy using these resources as much as we enjoyed writing it for you.

Karen D. Wood & Lina B. Soares

Table of Contents

Section I:

How Can I Integrate Comprehension Strategies?

One of the critical realities for many middle grades students is that very often they are not able to understand the central focus of learning contained in their content area text. In turn, this lack of understanding impedes their comprehension of the central focus and the key concepts presented in a unit of study. *Comprehension* is the ability to construct meaning, and *reading comprehension* is the ability to construct meaning from texts (Vacca, Vacca, & Mraz, 2013). While the term *reading comprehension* seems straightforward, the actual process that students employ to translate words into meaning is complex and requires students to interact with the text, to draw upon prior knowledge and experiences, and to consider the context in which the content is presented (Vacca, Vacca, & Mraz, 2013). As a result, the reader, the text, and the context are all integral components in the reading process, and each one affects how well young adolescents comprehend their reading material.

Teaching with texts requires middle grades teachers to recognize that, in truth, they are teachers of textual comprehension and that reading in a content area classroom requires students to employ a unique set of skills to understand each discipline. Today, we refer to this application as content area literacy or disciplinary literacy, and thus, instruction for content area literacy needs to be part of the content curriculum (Shanahan & Shanahan, 2008).

The literacy tools people use for communicating and learning constitute a thread common to learning in all disciplines. Middle grades students must be able to read, write, listen, speak, view, and visually represent information in every content area. With the volume of information students must learn, teachers cannot possibly tell them or read to them everything they need to know. They must, instead, help their students become self-directed learners, enabling them to take control of their own learning—a highly motivating experience essential for knowledge building (Guthrie, 2007). In addition, the Common Core State Standards (CCSS) place further emphasis on the importance of teaching students to read complex informational texts independently to build knowledge in history/social studies, science, and technical subjects (CCSS, 2010).

Implementing literacy strategies in the content areas can be a difficult and complex undertaking. Middle grades teachers face many constraints that hinder the use of literacy practices as tools for learning. With a predominant focus on content knowledge and so little time in which to teach, many content area teachers are reluctant to invest in instructional practices that appear to be too time-consuming or unrelated to their immediate purpose. It is not a wonder that many middle grades teachers ask. ***How can I integrate comprehension instruction in my discipline area?***

This section provides strategies for maximizing student motivation by incorporating meaningful ways to engage them in the learning process. The field of literacy has long recognized the relationship between vocabulary development and comprehension (Anderson & Freebody, 1981; Baumann, 2005; Blachowicz, Baumann, Manyak & Graves, 2015). It also emphasizes the importance of allowing students to self-select their assignments and their reading by first having accessible texts within the classroom environment and also by providing a menu of choices. The section includes activities that encourage group and pair interaction that meet young adolescents' social needs, as well as visual activities that provide alternative ways of learning and responding to text to meet the needs of diverse learners and students of all ability levels (Wood, Lapp, Flood & Taylor, 2008; Wood, Stover, Pilioneta & Taylor, 2013).

Think-Tac-Toe

Think-Tac-Toe (Samblis, 2006) uses a structure similar to a Tic-Tac-Toe board. The boards can include before-reading, during-reading, and after-reading activities that foster deeper interaction with text to enhance students' comprehension. The use of Think-Tac-Toe creates a balance between teacher-selected activities and student-selected activities. The parameters developed by the teacher ensure academically significant and rigorous activities.

Goal. These activities integrate writing skills, speaking and listening skills, collaboration, and the use of technology—all of which are expectations in the Common Core State Standards (CCSS, 2010).

Benefits. As young adolescents transition to being more like adults, they want to feel more self-worth and a stronger sense of autonomy— to do things independently. This strategy is developmentally appropriate due to the multitude of choices it provides. The strategy gives students ownership of their learning by allowing them to make decisions about their learning and engagement. It also provides teachers with a better understanding of their students' learning styles, interests, and strengths based on the activities selected by the students and the open-ended nature of the work.

Teacher Actions. Teachers can write Think-Tac-Toes specifically for a given text such as a textbook, class novel, or online articles, or they can construct them in an open-ended manner to coordinate with a particular genre that students are reading independently. Figure 1 is a sample seventh grade language arts Think-Tac-Toe one teacher created for the book *The Hunger Games* (Collins, 2008).

Figure 1. *Sample Think-Tac-Toe for Language Arts*

THE HUNGER GAMES **THINK-TAC-TOE**		
Directions. Choose a total of three activities to complete.		
Create a map of the setting for *The Hunger Games*. Include text features such as captions, labels, and a legend.	Write a letter from the perspective of one character to another character.	Choose three characters and explain what poem you think they would carry in their pockets and why.
Create a digital or print comic strip to retell the events from *The Hunger Games*.	FREE SPACE You create an activity to develop and support your reading.	Create a digital book trailer to promote *The Hunger Games*.
Choose one of the main characters, such as Katniss or Peeta, and create interview questions and the character's responses.	Create an artistic depiction to represent the main theme(s) in the book. Provide a written summary describing your artistic representation.	Write and deliver a speech explaining the author's purpose and the themes of the book. Provide sufficient reasons and evidence from the text to support your claim.

Student Actions. Students choose three tasks from the nine cells to explore the key ideas and concepts. As in typical tic-tac-toe games, the three activities may be chosen from a horizontal row, vertical row, or a diagonal row, giving students a set of choices that will include a variety of activities.

Differentiation. Teachers can easily adapt this strategy to meet a range of learner needs. Figure 2 is a Think-Tac-Toe board developed by a seventh grade biology teacher to engage her students in the study of sea turtle conservation and barrier island ecology. In this example, the teacher planned activities that would engage her students in collaborative discussions, interpreting information presented in digital images, citing evidence to support claims, and integrating math skills her students were learning in their seventh grade math curriculum.

Figure 2. *Sample Think-Tac-Toe That Provides a Variety of Challenges to Meet Students' Needs.*

SEA TURTLES THINK-TAC-TOE		
Directions. Choose a total of three activities to complete.		
Chart the specific ocean waters on a map where the five species of sea turtles nest and feed, and color code by species.	Describe the likely predators that often destroy turtle nests and locate an image using the Internet to illustrate the depredation.	Develop a collaborative multimedia project on how you may participate in sea turtle conservation.
Create a brochure of the five species of sea turtles to distribute at school. Provide the scientific name, characteristics, adaptations, habitat, and nesting range for each species.	**FREE SPACE** Create an activity to develop and support your reading.	Consult the following website to understand how sea turtles navigate, then explain to a classmate the concepts of magnetism and imprinting. http://www. conserveturtles.org/ seaturtleinformation. php?page=behavior
Create a PowerPoint presentation on the numerous hazards, both natural and man-made, that sea turtles face.	Build a model of a loggerhead to demonstrate your understanding of the anatomy. The model should be built to scale to represent the actual parts of the body.	Create a poster on the life history of the leatherback sea turtle. Include their habitat, diet, nesting habits, and other interesting facts.

Accessible Texts

The term *accessible text* is often used interchangeably with the more familiar term *leveled reading*. Accessible texts are quality, well-written books and passages of high interest to students and most importantly, match students' reading levels.

Goal. Match students to appropriate texts. Texts that are too difficult to read will not support learning for anyone at any age. Even with teacher support, some school texts can be beyond the reach of some students, and requiring them to read such texts leads to frustration and low self-efficacy, with little or no learning occurring. Students cannot learn from texts they cannot read.

Benefits. When students are matched to appropriate texts, the material becomes more relevant and meaningful.

Teacher Actions. After careful assessment of students' reading levels, middle grades teachers can differentiate the reading material by providing the highest level text students can comprehend without the frustration that comes from complex textbooks. For example, Figure 3 provides an overview of the multiple forms of texts teachers could use to teach the Holocaust.

Figure 3. *Sample Text Set for the Holocaust*

PICTURE BOOKS

Bunting E. (1993). *Terrible Things. An Allegory of the Holocaust.* New York, NY. The Jewish Publication Society.

Using an allegory to describe the Holocaust, Bunting depicts animals as Jewish people and others who suffered as a result of the Holocaust. The message teaches the reader to stand up for what one believes in and not to be prejudiced against others.

Hesse, K. (2004). *The cats in Krasinski Square.* New York, NY. Scholastic.

Two sisters who escaped the Warsaw ghetto befriend the many cats abandoned by their Jewish families. The cats help the girls discover holes in the Ghetto walls to help smuggle food to those still in the ghetto. When the soldiers find out about the plan, the cats play an instrumental role in helping the girls continue with their plan.

Innocenti, R. (1990). *Rose Blanche.* Mankato, MN. Creative Education Incorporated.

Rose witnesses the occupation of German soldiers in her own small town in Germany. Curiously, Rose follows one of the military trucks until she comes across a barbed wire fence corralling hungry children in striped uniforms. For the next several weeks, Rose returns with bread for the hungry children. One day she returns to find that the camp is empty. Suddenly, a shot is fired and Rose never returns home.

Johnson, T. (2004). *The harmonica.* Watertown, MA. Charlesbridge.

When Nazi soldiers separate a Jewish family by taking them away to a concentration camp, the son smuggles in a harmonica that was a gift from his father. The harmonica becomes his solace in the camp. When the commandant learns of his music, he orders him to play on command. While the soldiers do not demonstrate a sense of humanity, other Jews in the camp hear the music and find it comforting.

Polacco, P. (2009). *The butterfly.* New York, NY. Penguin Group.

In this true story of the author's aunt, Monique recounts her experience growing up in France during WWII. When Monique's French village is occupied by the Nazi soldiers, she meets a young Jewish girl, Sevrine, who has been hiding in her basement. The two become friends, but when Sevrine's family is discovered, they must flee.

Figure 3. *Continued*

GRAPHIC NOVELS
Spiegelman, A. (1993). *Maus. A survivor's tale. I. My father bleeds history. II. And here comes trouble again.* **New York, NY. Pantheon.** The author recounts the removal of his parents from their home in Warsaw to concentration camps including Auschwitz and Birkenau. While they all survived the horrific experience, Spiegelman describes the suffering his family endured in an attempt to comprehend how these experiences shaped his parents and his challenging relationship with his father. The author uses little mice to represent Jews and towering cats for the Nazi soldiers.

CHAPTER BOOKS
Boyne, J. (2006). *The boy in striped pajamas.* **New York, NY: David Fickling Books.** Bruno's family moves due to his father's job promotion with his job during WWII in Nazi Germany. Bruno, young, adventurous, and curious, explores the area around the new house and comes across a barbed wire fence separating him from another young boy wearing striped pajamas. This new friend faces different circumstances than Bruno, and, ultimately, their friendship has devastating consequences.
Lowry, L. (1989). *Number the stars.* **New York, NY: Houghton Mifflin.** Annemarie's family disguises her best friend as a member of the family when the Germans invade Copenhagen in 1943. As part of the Danish resistance movement, Annemarie's family engages in a dangerous mission to smuggle slaves to safety in Sweden.

Texts that are too difficult to read will not support learning for anyone at any age. If a book is far beyond a reader's capability, even support from a more knowledgeable other may not be enough to make it productive for learning. Even with teacher support, school texts can sometimes be beyond the reach of some students, and requiring them to read such texts leads to frustration and low self-esteem, with little or no learning occurring. Students need opportunities to acquire the necessary reading skills and content in their specific subject areas. The use of accessible texts in the middle grade classroom provides middle grade students the reading comfort they need, while offering a balance between teacher support and challenge.

Accessible Text Sets

Goal. Use a collection of multiple resources, known as *text sets* to provide a range of reading material unified by a particular topic, theme, or concept and include a variety of genres and reading levels to meet the diverse experiences, interests, and reading abilities of adolescent readers.

Benefits. Experiencing the topic through multiple text types affects comprehension by reinforcing vocabulary and concept development for English language learners and struggling readers (Young & Hadaway, 2006). Text sets have also been shown to allow readers to organize information such that readers can draw connections across texts (Lehman, 2007). Texts sets allow readers of varying reading levels to engage in content-specific materials and apply their reading strategies, such as cause and effect, prediction, drawing conclusions, and sequencing events because the sets are organized for a broad range of reading levels.

Teacher Actions. Teachers create text sets that may include print and digital genres such as narratives, nonfiction, charts, maps, timelines, primary sources, photographs, poetry, song lyrics, letters, journals, and graphic novels. The goal is to provide a balance between whole group instruction, small group discussion, and independent reading that is best achieved through a structured management program such as the Reading Workshop format (Frey & Fisher, 2006).

The Reading Workshop consists of four essential phases that permits classroom teachers to demonstrate explicit instruction through modeling and guided practice and then provide opportunities for their students to try techniques on their own through collaborative practice, independent practice, and application. This gradual release of responsibility (Pearson & Gallagher, 1983) allows teachers to move from teacher-centered discussions (explicit instruction and modeling), in which they control the flow of activity, to shared stances (scaffolding and coaching), in which responsibility is more equally shared, to more student-centered stances (facilitating and participation) in which students take primary responsibility. The Reading Workshop can be easily adapted to content area classrooms.

1. Focus lessons introduce new concepts and learning objectives. Teachers model and think aloud to demonstrate the learning objective rather than simply explaining. In doing so, teachers build important metacognitive skills students need to increase comprehension.

2. Guided instruction involves carefully scaffolded teacher instruction. Under the teacher's guidance, this is a time for students to practice new concepts and learning objectives.

3. Collaborative learning is a time to initiate collective inquiry, collaboration, and communication from which students are able to make purposeful, conscious choices when finding solutions to problems, answers to their questions, and decisions regarding their reading content as they work to co-construct meaning.

4. Independent work involves giving students time to practice new skills and apply new content in different ways.

The workshop model is an effective way of engaging students in the study of content in academic disciplines and literature. It is an excellent tool teachers can use to model new skills and scaffold instruction so students become independent readers, writers, and thinkers.

See Appendix A for the CCSS list of Exemplar Texts for Grades 6–8.

Rereading Strategies

Rereading is a long-standing, effective instructional practice that serves a variety of purposes.

Goal. Provide strategies to motivate students to reread and return to the text to build fluency and improve comprehension.

Benefits. As Tovani (2004) explained, "Good readers reread and return to text to build and extend their knowledge of specific concepts, or to enhance their enjoyment of texts they have enjoyed previously" (p. 21). Furthermore, repeated readings of the same text promote fluency as students become more efficient in accurately recognizing words, such as high frequency words, and in increasing their reading rate (Gunning, 2012). Rereading also has a place in content area instruction to clarify information in class discussions, to find new facts, to develop appreciation for conceptual ideas, and even to broaden understanding.

Teacher Actions.

Close Reading. One way teachers can promote purposeful rereading is by using close reading. Given the extraordinary amount of informational texts presented in print and digital formats that students encounter in today's classrooms, the need for students to engage in critical reading to determine what a text says explicitly is essential for students to become critical consumers of information. In addition, the Common Core State Standards (CCSS) place further emphasis on the importance of teaching students to engage in "close, attentive reading" as critical text analysis relates to 80% of the Reading standards at each grade level (CCSS, 2010).

Close reading is the process of understanding how the words on a page fit together to support the author's central ideas (Cummins, 2012). It is a tool to teach students to preview a text, make predictions about the author's central ideas, and then read with a sustained purpose to understand the author's words. The beauty of this strategy lies in its application. Students are taught to question while reading, pause and summarize as they read, and to monitor their understanding of the reading material. The process increases comprehension because students continually reread a passage while taking notes to get a true understanding of what the author is saying. In other words, students begin with the smallest unit of meaning—words—and then examine sentences, and paragraphs to capture the central ideas. Fisher and Frey (2012) posit that "close reading should be accompanied by purposeful, scaffolded instruction about the passage" (p. 8) which means that teachers and students are involved in the close reading strategy (see Figure 4).

Figure 4. *Student and Teacher Actions in Close Reading*

STUDENTS' ACTIONS	TEACHERS' ACTIONS
Read with a pencil	Reads aloud confusing parts
Question	Models how to think out loud
Reread	Asks text-dependent questions
Look for evidence	Coaches students to ask questions
Provide evidence	Teaches students to annotate
Discuss the reading with peers	Teaches students to cite evidence

Reaction Review Guide. One way teachers can promote purposeful, engaged rereading is by using a type of "statement guide" called the Reaction Review Guide (Wood, Lapp, Flood, & Taylor, 2008). As the name implies, these guides use statements instead of questions to get students to think about, discuss, share, and reflect on key concepts from a text selection. Further, the guides give teachers the opportunity to see cognitive growth in students because they typically span the pre-reading, reading, and post-reading stages of a lesson. The Reaction Review Guide improves comprehension through the practice of rereading and the exchange of ideas as students hear comments of their peers. This interaction permits students to co-construct meaning.

Teacher Actions. Provide statements related to a text selection that span the pre-reading, reading, and post-reading stages of a lesson.

Student Actions. Prior to reading, students respond to the statements in the guide with a partner or small group, contributing their thinking and prior knowledge about each statement. Then, they use the statements to guide and focus their attention while reading. Afterward, they return to discuss what they have learned by referring back to the related parts of the targeted text (i.e., rereading).

The Reaction Review Guide is particularly suited for mathematics instruction because learning mathematics often involves the introduction of new concepts for which students may have little prior knowledge (Wood, Lapp, Flood, & Taylor, 2008). Teachers frequently comment on the difficulty of getting students to reread and refer to their mathematics textbooks to answer questions they have or to refresh their memories about how to solve computation problems. The guide in Figure 5 provides an opportunity for students to justify their thinking when they determine whether mathematical statements are correct according to what they have just studied. The Reaction Review Guide should precede any individual classroom test to allow pairs of students to review, process, share, and confirm their new learning.

Figure 5. *Sample Reaction Review Guide Applied to Mathematics*

USING PERCENTAGES IN EVERYDAY LIFE

Directions. With your partner, take turns reading each statement below and discuss possible responses. Indicate if you agree or disagree but be sure to go back to your text and related materials to support and explain your answer, just as we did together in class. Use examples whenever appropriate and tell how you came up with that.

1. **A percentage is a way of representing a fraction.**
   I agree _____ x _____ I disagree _____ because.
   on page 96 of our book it said that. We learned that the fraction has a denominator of 100. So 25% would be 25/100 which means one fourth.

2. **You can think of a percentage as meaning "out of 100."**
   I agree _____ x _____ I disagree _____ because.
   it also said that in the book and in class (See statement number 1). So 6% tax added to 100 pennies ($1.00) would be $1.06.

3. **A sales tax of 7% means that for every dollar something costs, a person would need to pay seven times more.**
   I agree _____ x _____ I disagree _____ because.
   the person would have to pay 7 cents not seven times more. It would look like this. $1.00 + (7% of 1.00) = $1.00 + .07 =$1.07.

4. **If the state sales tax is 6%, the total cost of the $30.00 shirt is $36.00.**
   I agree _____ x _____ I disagree _____ because.
   that is too much. You just multiply 6 x 30.00 which comes out to $1.80, so the total price would be $31.80.

5. **Lunch was $15.00 and with the 20% tip, it was $18.00.**
   I agree _____ x _____ I disagree _____ because.
   it is easy to determine 10%, which would be $1.50. So then you just add another 10%, which makes it $3.00. $15.00 + $3.00 = $18.00

6. **Knowing how to calculate percentages is essential in everyday life.**
   I agree _____ x _____ I disagree _____ because.
   we talked about doing percentages to figure out tips in restaurants. Also when something you want to buy is on sale, you need to figure out how much it will cost. You need to know percentages if you are doing a survey to find out about something.

Retelling in Flexible Groups

When students read texts that are easy or at their independent levels, very little instructional support is needed for them to comprehend the texts. On the other hand, most texts used in content classrooms are at many students' instructional reading levels or even frustration levels, and it sometimes becomes necessary for teachers to demonstrate and model a new strategy for students and then give them the opportunity to work in groups, pairs, and individually to master the strategy.

Goal. The Phased Transfer Model of Instruction with flexible grouping (in small groups or pairs) (Wood, 2002; Wood, Lapp, Flood, & Taylor, 2008) can be used in any subject area or grade level to teach particular skills and strategies. Figure 6 is a generic illustration of the model.

Benefits. The grouping element provides the social support necessary for sharing knowledge, and is developmentally appropriate for middle schoolers. Building on middle grades students need to be social (Brown & Knowles, 2007), students benefit from reading in a small group setting under the guidance of their teacher. As students begin to think out loud what they are reading in conjunction with their peers, they gradually begin to retell, put information in their own words, and then record their own words in print or a digital format.

The chart in Figure 6 is an illustration of how the Phased Transfer Model with Flexible Grouping is a process for releasing instructional responsibility to students, assigning them to work collaboratively to assimilate the new learning. It begins with a whole class teacher explanation, purpose-setting, and demonstration, then the students work in pairs or small groups to practice the skill/strategy, content, or lesson while the teacher circulates to assist, monitor, and answer questions. Next, they use the new skill/strategy on their own and lastly apply it to new contexts independently.

Figure 6. *Phased Transfer Model of Instruction with Flexible Grouping*

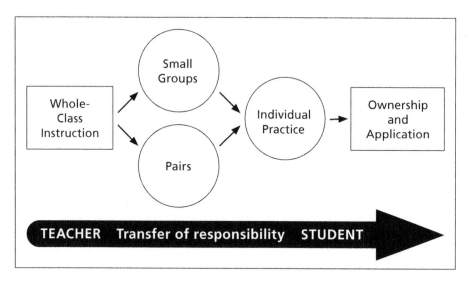

Figure 7 gives a step-by-step procedure for applying the model to a classroom setting. The example describes the process of teaching students how to retell, put information in their own words, and then put their oral retelling in print form as a summary of the content read (e.g., digital or print text), viewed (e.g., a science experiment), or heard (e.g., a lecture or explanation).

Figure 7. *Phased Transfer Model Lesson Description*

GENERIC PROCEDURES FOR THE PHASED TRANSFER MODEL APPLICABLE TO ANY LESSON

- The lesson begins with the teacher showing an example of the finished product, an exemplar of what the students should achieve.

- (In other instances, this could be a series of predictions, a descriptive paragraph, a final research project, etc.)

- Then the teacher and the students analyze the product, looking at the features and how it represents the selection read in a succinct manner. (All the examples and passages used are related to the science topics under study to further enhance learning.)

- Next, the teacher displays a passage and thinks aloud how to summarize and put the information in her own words to illustrate the invisible thought processes for the class.

- The teacher displays an additional passage and, together with the students, comes up with an oral and then a written retelling of the content, discussing why they left out certain information to get to the main points.

- At this point, the students are asked to work in their pre-assigned groups (preferably heterogeneous) to contribute to an additional retelling of passage content. The grouping allows the teacher to circulate, monitor, assist, and assess whether additional practice is needed.

- After feeling that the groups are ready to move into pairs, the teacher again asks them to engage in a retelling of the content of a new passage. This paired arrangement is repeated until the teacher determines the students are ready to move to the independent practice phase.

- The final two phases involve individual practice and then illustrating how to apply the new learning to other subject areas.

Graphic Aids

Although graphic aids often contain essential information for an extended understanding of the content under study, many students simply skip maps, charts, and graphs in print or digital text. Authors include graphics to condense, expand, or elaborate on key concepts. In fact, the Common Core State Standards include the need to help students "integrate visual information (e.g., in charts, graphs, photographs, videos, or maps) with other information in print and digital texts" (CCSS, 2010, RH.6–8.7).

The ability to gain knowledge from information that is observed and not "read" in the conventional sense is termed *visual literacy,* and it is one of the five communication processes. reading, writing, listening, speaking, and viewing (Flood, Heath, & Lapp, 2007; Wood, Stover, Pilonieta, & Taylor, 2012).

Benefits. While strategy guides such as the Reading Road Map can take substantial time to develop, they can be used year after year, modified as new information becomes available, and shared with other teachers. In addition, they can be used to emphasize varied facets of reading, such as drawing conclusions, predicting, inferring, critical analysis, vocabulary development, and concept learning. The end goal of any instructional routine is for students to become strategic, independent learners. Strategy guides are one way to foster this independence as students emerge more metacognitively aware of how to gain information from multiple sources of content.

Teacher Actions. Teachers support visual literacy by designing strategy guides or graphic aids to guide students through the reading of multiple sources of material related to the topic studied. They can consist of combinations of activities such as questions, statements, or manipulatives. Well-designed strategy guides can serve as "tutors in print form," directing students to multiple sources of information while simultaneously guiding them to the most important content.

Student Actions. Students write, chart, diagram, create flow charts, graphic organizers or draw their responses individually, with partners, or as groups.

Reading Road Map Example. To help students develop strategic reading skills and the use of graphic aids in textbooks and online sources in social studies, the Reading Road Map strategy guide (Wood, Lapp, Flood, & Taylor, 2008) takes students on a journey through a text using a road map format, directing them to slow down, speed up, or skip certain textual sites along the way.

Appendix B provides a full lesson based on the Reading Road Map.

In a typical Reading Road Map, students are taken strategically through a variety of texts, including the textbook, as well as additional sources such as websites. The text is strategically broken into sections to chunk the reading, and students are provided with a clear reading purpose with suggestions for varying their reading rate. Guides are designed with *location information*—page numbers along with headings or subheadings taken from the text selection—to show students the exact section of the text or visual aid they should read. *Images or signs* provide students with direction about how to read that section of text or related material. For instance, students may be asked to slow down to focus on specific content, skim sections to get a broad idea of information, work with another student, or stop to respond to text through discussion or writing. These images support students as they read a variety of texts and show them the importance of reading flexibly—sometimes slowly and sometimes quickly—skimming and scanning depending on the text and purpose for reading. They also serve as visual cues to students about the active nature of reading. The images inserted are usually produced in a word processing program using clip art or images obtained from free or royalty-free websites or other sources.

Predicting

Getting students to predict what will occur in a text is a widely accepted means of focusing their attention on the content to be read, thereby improving their understanding of the key concepts (Fisher & Frey, 2012). Yet, in order to make predictions about a text, students must have prior knowledge or experiences about the topic and a means or a reason to retrieve this latent information and knowledge. Getting students to make predictions about a text is more than just giving the directive to "guess what will happen in this story." It seems likely that some sort of triggering of the imagination—a retrieval of images of previous experiences—is necessary to ensure adequate predictions and to motivate students to read the text to follow.

Imagine, Elaborate, Predict, Confirm. One way teachers can get students to make predictions about text is the Imagine, Elaborate, Predict, and Confirm or IEPC strategy (Wood & Endres 2002; Wood, Stover, & Taylor, in press). Designed to motivate students' interest in reading while simultaneously enhancing their ability to comprehend and write descriptively, IEPC is a whole-class strategy designed to take the predictive process back to its origins in the imagination and extend it.

1. **I**magining is a critical aspect of good comprehension (RAND Reading Study Group, 2002). Students imagine using a strategy that activates their five senses (seeing, hearing, smelling, tasting, and physically or emotionally feeling).

2. **E**laboration. Students form connections between previously learned information and new content through imagery and visualization, analogies, descriptions, and details (Anderson & Armbruster, 1984). Because students typically do not offer extended responses without encouragement, teachers strategically demonstrate, model, or prompt

students with extra-textual questions or questions that prompt students to make connections beyond the information in the text by drawing upon their prior knowledge.

3. **P**rediction. Students use their prior knowledge to anticipate what may occur in a reading selection. When students make predictions, they are developing a purpose for reading. Prediction is an essential instructional element that helps direct and motivate the reader to get started, stay on course, and proceed to the end of the reading assignment. The process of prediction becomes a method for students to set their own purposes for reading, to question these predictions, and to read for further proof and evidence (Wood & Endres, 2004; Wood, Stover, & Taylor, in press).

4. **C**onfirmation. Students read to verify predictions.

These research-based elements, advocated in the professional literature for decades, make up the Imagine, Elaborate, Predict, and Confirm (IEPC) strategy. Appendix C details procedures for its classroom use.

Ten Important Words Plus

Description. Easily integrated into any content area, Ten Important Words Plus (Yopp & Yopp, 2007) challenges students to sift through and pare down all of the information presented in the text and forces students to interact with key vocabulary, examine how words connect to the text, and synthesize the information to get the big idea. Students experience the words in meaningful contexts and participate in rich conversations with their peers.

Goal. Improves vocabulary knowledge of words in isolation as well as in the context of the reading by giving students multiple exposures to the word in meaningful context

Benefits. Students determine which words will be chosen for study giving them a sense of ownership and stake in their own learning; self-selection and having a voice and choice in learning activities motivates and engages students of all ability levels (Dunston & Gambrell, 2009; Wood, Harmon, Kissel, & Hedrick, 2011). In sum, using the *Ten Important Words Plus* strategy across content areas such as science allows students to engage more deeply with the text and increase their understanding of key vocabulary, resulting in improved comprehension. Through multiple exposures and interactions with the words, students engage in reading, recording, discussing, writing, and thinking about words in alternative ways to extend their knowledge. Students can also practice their graphing skills as they tally and represent the key terms.

Teacher Actions. The teacher models the steps of the strategy with a thinkaloud using an excerpt of the online text. After reading the excerpt of online text, the teacher demonstrates how to select key words from the selection. By thinking aloud about the words and reasons for selecting them, the teacher gives an explicit example of how to purposely choose important words. Then the teacher models how to make a one-sentence summary of the reading using the selected words.

Student Actions. Students read the remainder of the online text and select ten words they think are most important to the selection and record each word on a sticky note. Then students post their words on a class bar graph, compiling common words in the same column. They then discuss the patterns they find in their choices and how frequently specific words occur.

Figure 8. *Photo of Graph of 10 Important Words in Science*

The class then discusses the selected words and their significance to the online text. Next, using the words from the graph, the students write a one-sentence summary of the entire passage.

The extension or "Plus" aspect of the Ten Important Words Plus technique engages students in a deeper analysis and interaction with the words. Working in small groups, students use color-coded task cards with prompts to examine the vocabulary on the bar graph in more depth and to promote deeper word learning. Tasks such as these require students to find synonyms, identify antonyms, and generate sentences using the words, or list different forms of the words.

Appendix D details using Ten Important Words Plus strategy to increase students' understanding of content area vocabulary and improve their comprehension of science text during a unit on the human body systems.

Extension Opportunity. Creating a semantic map (a graphic representation) allows students to increase their vocabulary knowledge as they organize their vocabulary words in categories or by concepts. Other extensions are drawing a picture, acting out the word, and finding other examples of the use of a particular word. After students complete the given task using a word from the bar graph, they either select a new word and perform the same activity or choose a different task. However, it is beneficial for students to engage in the same task using different words to build their competency in the particular skill. If time allows, ask students to share their work with the class and add the new content area words to their personal dictionaries and a class word wall to enhance their word knowledge.

Research Process

To emphasize the significant role research plays towards building comprehension, it is important to consider the higher-level thinking skills that are required to conduct research. For example, students formulate a research project, design the activities, synthesize information from multiple sources, analyze information to make informed decisions, and create products and personalized representations of their understanding. These higher order cognitive skills are needed for students to engage in researching a topic and learning more about the topic.

Goal. In one week, students produce a brief but strong research paper. The skill set learned could transfer to any content area and would have real-life connections.

Benefits. Writing a research paper gives students practice in innovation and problem solving, while students improve their communication literacy in the core subject areas. It is developmentally appropriate because the instruction is scaffolded and the students have autonomy in selecting topics.

Teacher Actions. Core subject teachers integrate information, media, and technology skills into goals and objectives of a research paper required in English Language Arts curriculum. Make the task sequential and student-driven.

Example. A three-person team led by a language arts teacher. The team includes a science and math teacher, and each of the three teach a daily social studies class. The paper will have a science focus, and can, after completed, serve as the roadmap for the traditional science fair entry.

Procedure for Teaching Students Research Process.

1. **Use modified KWL** to create student awareness of the many times that they informally rely on data and research to make decisions about purchasing video games or deciding what to wear or which movie to see.

    a. Students brainstorm questions that they are curious about. What sort of careers are available to video game designers? How common is school bullying in our state? What effect does texting have on writing skills? What fashions are popular in Europe and how much do American teenagers influence those styles?

    b. After one round of narrowing the topics, the class chooses one of the topics to investigate. They then record their ideas in a modified KWL chart, which uses a confirming step to determine the varied sources of the content. (Here's what I *think* I **K**now. This is what I **W***ant to find out. And, at completion of the work, this is what I* **L***earned by confirming* it using multiple sources).

    c. Using the middle column labeled *What We Want to Find Out,* on a Smart Board the teacher models some general research skills via the Internet. The class progressively takes control of the process as they learn how to determine the value of an article or website and what information is critical to the topic (as opposed to what is non-essential).

    d. The teacher assesses students' mastery of choosing a topic, determining two or three core questions, and then selecting the most critical information with sources cited.

2. **Use daybooks to document the research paper assignment.** Throughout the year, in science class, students use daybooks to organize all of their thinking and ideas. Each student builds his or her daybook with a table of contents and numbered pages, glued-in handouts, sketches of lab experiments and bright colors, a section for their growing vocabulary, and even an ongoing list of grades from

their various assessments. In the daybook, students begin to document their research paper assignment.

a. Students respond in a variety of ways to strategies for integrating writing and higher order thinking. Figure 9 shows a sample daybook excerpt using the 3-2-1 strategy (Zygouris-Coe, Wiggins, & Smith, 2004) in which students write about 3 things they discovered, 2 things they found interesting and 1 question they still have about the selection.

Figure 9. *Sample Daybook Entry-Science Topic. Global Warming*

Let's use a 3, 2, 1 review in our discussion today. Glue this handout in you science daybook and record these things.

3 things you learned about global warming today

2 interesting facts

1 question that you still have

I learned this today.

1. The earth is hot and getting hotter!

2. Greenhouse gases are a big part of the reason why. This is brought on by burning fossil fuels and cutting down the rainforests.

b. The class broadly reviews the curriculum topics that they have covered to that point, and the science teacher reviews several interesting news events related to science. After briefly discussing each, the students select a broad topic (such as global warming) as a common point of interest. Next, they use their science daybooks to individually record facts from the class conversation. In a whole class discussion format, they brainstorm questions that they are interested in investigating. Finally, they share their potential research questions with the class to either consolidate them or eliminate their overlap.

c.   In the computer lab, the class reads more on these questions and subtopics that, when pooled, would lead to a great deal of information about the topic. This initial step of reading in general is important because, as the teacher explains earlier, if they can find all of the answers to their research questions quickly, then they need to select another subtopic to explore.

3.   **One teacher sets up a class Wiki** to help manage the group's growing base of content information on the selected topic. In their routine general writing, students use the Wiki for their research project; this includes student writing groups and a full implementation of process writing. Students work individually or within their writing groups to gather information, share it on the Wiki, discuss it there electronically, and eventually return to their science daybooks or electronic files for a careful crafting of the first draft of their papers.

4.   **The ELA and science teachers continually monitor the process and results.** The ELA class includes daily mini-lessons on topics relevant to the students' immediate work. summarizing an article, keeping a running list of citations for those articles, taking effective notes on topics emerging from the reading, tracking information to be certain that it is tightly focused on the selected subtopic, and finally, using writing groups for conferencing on the growing draft. The science teacher works daily with the students, providing feedback on both the paper's development and its content. In addition, the science teacher fosters the excitement that comes from testing theories, which students would soon do through their data-based science fair projects.

Big 6 Model of Research

Another strategy to improve comprehension in young adults is the Big 6 Model of Research. It increases comprehension by requiring students to define a task, seek and search information, analyze the information to be used, and develop a final product.

As students work through the challenging approach with complex tasks, they define the tasks, seek information, locate resources, use information, synthesize information, and evaluate information.

Benefits. Students use higher order thinking skills, synthesize information from multiple sources, analyze information to make informed decisions, and create products and personalized representations of their understanding. It is particularly appropriate for young adolescents because it uses the discovery approach, which allows students self-direction and autonomy. It connects to real-life situations and challenges students to solve real world problems. Students work collaboratively in devising approaches and finding solutions.

Teacher Actions. In a math class struggling with calculating percents of numbers, the teacher asked her students, "Where do we see percentages in real life?" Students came up with a multitude of responses, such as the mall, the bank, restaurants, advertisements on TV, at school, and in the grocery store. The teacher then described the project.

For this project you will find percentages in real life and then write multi-step tasks about these percentages. We will post all of these tasks on the Internet, and then you will pick some of your classmates' tasks to solve. Make sure that your tasks are realistic.

Student Actions. To find real-world examples of percentages, students used the Big 6 research strategy (for more information see www.big6.com). Figure 10 defines each task and illustrates how it was applied to mathematics during the project.

Figure 10. *Big 6 Model of Research Applied to Mathematics*

STRATEGY	DESCRIPTION	EXAMPLE IN THIS LESSON
Defining the task	Students identify what the task is and what is expected of them.	Each of the students reread the project requirements and discussed their tasks
Seeking information	Students determine where to go to seek information and begin to search for information.	Students decided that the Internet and newspaper advertisements would both have examples of percentages in real life.
Locating resources	Students locate resources to help them complete the task.	Students used the Internet or newspaper advertisements to find examples of percentages in real life.
Using information	Students read and examine information to become familiar with what they find.	Students examined examples of percentages that they found online or in newspapers.
Synthesizing information	Students combine the information that they found in search of main ideas and commonalities or frequently occurring topics	Students create tasks that use the information that they found about percentages in real-life and posted the tasks on the class website or wiki.

Evaluating information	Students reexamine the information that they have synthesized to determine. 1) if they have enough information to complete the task, 2) how to complete the task, 3) what conclusions to draw based on the information that they synthesized.	Students solved their classmates' tasks and posted strategies and solutions on the class website or wiki.

Students worked through the Big 6 process by defining the task, seeking information, locating resources, using information, and synthesizing and evaluating information. For example, Sarah had heard about credit cards and the interest rate percentage that people had to pay if they paid their credit card bills late. As a result, Sarah used the Internet to research typical credit card interest rates and what happens to people's bills if they don't pay on time. Sarah then synthesized her information and wrote the task, "If you owe $1,000 in credit card bills, how much money do you end up paying if you only pay the minimum payment each month rather than paying the bill off at one time?"

Teacher Action. In addition to the many facets of the wix, the class website, teachers used digital tools such as Voicethread (http://voicethread.com), in which students could record their voices telling the steps involved in solving a problem. For example, the teacher might divide the class in groups and assign each group a Voicethread link to various word problems in mathematics. Links may include certain questions such as "What do you need to know to begin solving this problem?" "Take turns recording your voice for each step needed to come up with the answer." Then we will listen to each group's method for solving the problem.

Student Actions. Students posted answers and solutions to the class wix, often blogging their responses with one another. In addition to posting their answer, students summarized their steps and defended their solutions by answering: "How would you explain to a friend how you solved this task? How would you prove that you have a correct solution?"

In summary, the Big 6 research model impacts comprehension because the research model allows students to apply a familiar framework that helps them research and analyze how percentages are important in real-life situations. Students use the information they find to create multistep tasks that involve percentages of quantities. Finally, developing a class wix to address various aspects of math allows students to share their tasks, approaches, and solutions with each other.

Integrated Literacy Circles

Integrated literacy circles are a text-based instructional strategy employed in middle grades classrooms today as a way to encourage students to talk about literature (Daniels, 1994, 2002). In addition, literacy circles have the potential to provide students with a forum from which to question as they read, to know the author's intent, and to understand the historical, social, cultural, and political influences in their lives (Beck, McKeown, Hamilton, & Kucan, 1997). Research has shown that student engagement in discussion about texts improves reading comprehension, higher-level thinking skills, and increased motivation (Gambrell, 2004; Soares, 2009). Moreover, literacy circles provide a space for student participation as a collaborative community of learners who work together to make meaning (Gee, 2000; Moll, 1990; Lave & Wenger, 1991).

In a middle school integrated literacy circle, students learn content under study as they apply, organize, and coordinate the skills and strategies needed for proficient reading. Teachers can use literacy circles to teach and reinforce students' understanding of literacy skills and tasks including predicting, sequencing, summarizing, skimming for main ideas, inferring, critical analysis, and text structure.

Benefits. Consequently, the circles provide a vehicle for teachers to scaffold the concepts to be learned while enabling peer groups to co-construct the information through discussion. Because students take ownership of the task and content, these reading lessons can be more meaningful and increase the likelihood that students will transfer their reading knowledge to other reading situations.

Teacher Actions. In a typical integrated literacy circles setting, the teacher assigns the students to small groups of five to eight to form "reading skill" circles. The teacher explains a particular reading task, skill, or strategy and thinks aloud to model the thought processes needed to accomplish the task. The text selected can be any length and from any source, online or traditional, as long as it is useful as a resource to learn the topic under study and can stimulate meaningful discussion.

Student Actions. Students complete a reading task alone, with others, or with the assistance of the teacher; then they discuss the results with their peer group members. Students ask for help from the teacher and others when necessary. The students discuss the reading, and after the discussion, the teacher assigns students additional material to read, with the purpose of coordinating and applying the knowledge to accomplish the task independently. Instruction on the task culminates in the students summarizing what they have learned about performing the target task—both the literacy skill and the content material. With her prompting, students discuss the knowledge they used and their understanding of how it was used. Students may also synthesize the contributions of other group and class members and revise their understanding of the task and how they might perform it better next time.

Phases of Instruction. The integrated literacy circles approach involves seven phases of instruction. exploration, explication, translation, modeling, guided practice, application, and closure (Blanton, Pilonieta, & Wood, 2007).

See Appendix E for a full lesson example of integrated literacy circles.

> **Exploration Phase.** Teacher elicits and probes students' prior knowledge about the reading task to be performed. Example. Who can tell me what "cause and effect" means?

> **Explication Phase.** Teacher explains (1) what the task is, (2) the procedures for the task and what knowledge is needed, and (3) when the knowledge can be applied and why.

Translation Phase. Students translate, or explain, the task in their own words to get evidence for judging how well students are interpreting and understanding the language needed for comprehending the task. For example, *Using your own words, who can tell me what a cause and effect relationship is?*

Modeling Phase. The teacher models and demonstrates, by thinking aloud, how the knowledge is coordinated to complete the task. This process makes implicit thinking processes explicit. Example. show them If... then examples on the board; then, have them as a class locate the causes and effects on a handout related to the topic under study.

Guided Practice Phase. Students work with partners or small groups to coordinate and enact the knowledge to accomplish the reading task. Each student's verbalizing of the thinking processes affects the thinking processes of the group, making learning evident to the teacher/observer. Example. Have students work in pairs to practice recognizing cause and effect.

Application Phase. Students independently accomplish the task they completed in the previous phases using new, but similar, material. Example. use web-based activities to which they could apply what they have learned.

Closure Phase. Students summarize what they have learned about performing the target task—both the literacy skill and the content material. Example. students discuss the knowledge they used and their understanding of how it was used. Students synthesize the contributions of other group and class members and revise their understanding of the task and how they might perform it better next time.

To help students reflect on how the lesson phases helped them understand both the content area concepts and the skills needed to fully comprehend those concepts, teachers can give them a Student Reaction/Reflection Form shown in Figure 11. Students need not complete reflections forms each time they participate in an integrated literacy circle. However, when they are learning a new skill, reflecting on the process and on the information learned will highlight key information for students, which, in turn, will help their comprehension.

Figure 11. *Student Reaction/Reflection Form for Integrated Literacy Circles*

The purpose of this form is to help you organize your thoughts and give you the opportunity to think back over the steps we went through as we explored the meaning of cause and effect. It can be very meaningful as a learner to jot down strategies that were helpful and reflect on the stages that helped you learn the concept of cause and effect. Work with your circle group as you reflect on the steps we took to understand our lessons.	
Explanation	The explanation helped us think about the relationships we read about in our textbooks. The explanation made us think out loud "what happened and why."
Procedures	The procedures we liked the most were highlighting and hunting for the signal words that alerted us to cause and effect.
Teacher Modeling	When our teacher modeled for us, it gave us a visual. The combination of seeing and copying what our teacher said and did, really gave us the fundamentals of cause and effect.
Guided Practice	Guided practice was the most helpful. We were able to identify even more examples of cause and effect while working together. It really helps to have another person who may see the relationship and then can help explain.
Application	This practice helped us because now we are able to see in our reading that there are concepts that talk about something happening and now we know to look for why.

Teachers and teacher educators share a common goal—they all strive to help their students become knowledgeable, lifelong learners. Language arts teachers want their students to become proficient readers and writers, to appreciate and understand quality works of literature, and to apply their literacy skills with all texts. Social studies teachers want their students to read and write like historians, to value primary sources of information, and to use this knowledge to understand the world around them and how we got here. Science teachers want their students to read and write like scientists, to understand how the world works, and to question things around them. Similarly, mathematics teachers want their students to read and write like mathematicians, develop skill in manipulating numerical data, and learn problem-solving skills applicable in the real world. Middle grades teachers will find that integrated literacy circles provide a thoughtful method to teach the necessary reading skills in the academic-specific areas as students read and explore content to be studied and topics of interest.

Summary

Adolescent learners of today represent a vast range of diverse needs and backgrounds in terms of cultural, socioeconomic, and linguistic characteristics. In today's world, they need to be able to analyze, interpret, examine, and communicate content about their print and non-print worlds in both academic and non-academic settings. Understanding the meaning of text in all its forms, words, paragraphs, numbers, gestural, and visual is the underlying goal of learning. In their Position Statement on Adolescent Literacy (www.reading. org/Resources/ResourcesbyTopic/Adolescent/Overview.aspx), the International Literacy Association states that "Adolescents continue to need general comprehension and study strategies that can be used across a broad range of texts… in all disciplines" (Draper, 2012). Similarly, many of the missions of the Association for Middle Level Education address these needs, particularly in the area of active learning. In *This We Believe. Keys to Educating Young Adolescents* (2010), it states. "Instructional practices place students at the center of the learning process. As they develop the ability to hypothesize, to organize information into useful and meaningful constructs, and to grasp long-term cause and effect relationships…"

This section featured strategies and sample lessons focused on the goal of understanding and comprehending digital and print text in all subject areas. These strategies were selected because they address the need to engage adolescents in active, engaged learning activities that promote comprehension through collaboration and conversation, hallmarks of the social needs of the adolescent learner.

Acknowledgements

Harmon, J. M., Keehn, S., Kenney, M. S., & Wood, K. D. (2005). A tutoring program for struggling adolescent readers. *Middle School Journal, 36*(3), 57–62.

Harmon, J. M., Wood, K. D., & Stover, K. (2012). Four components to promote literacy engagement in subject matter disciplines. *Middle School Journal, 44*(2), 49–57.

Lehman, B. (2007). *Children's literature and learning. Literary study across the curriculum.* New York: Teachers College Press.

Wood, K. D. (2001). Aiding comprehension with the imagine, elaborate, predict, and confirm (IEPC) strategy. *Middle School Journal, 33*(3), 47–54.

Wood, K. D., Jones, J., Stover, K., & Polly, D. (2011). STEM literacies. Integrating reading, writing, and technology in science and mathematics. *Middle School Journal, 43*(1), 55–62.

Wood, K. D., Pilonieta, P., & Blanton, W. E. (2009). Teaching content and skills through integrated literacy circles. *Middle School Journal, 41*(1), 56–62.

Wood, K. D., Stover, K., Pilonieta, P., & Taylor, B. (2012). Don't skip the graphics! Focusing students' attention on the visual aids in digital and traditional texts. *Middle School Journal, 43*(4), 60–68.

References

Anderson, R., & Freebody, P. (1981). Vocabulary knowledge. In J. T. Guthrie (Ed.), *Comprehension and teaching. Research reviews* (pp. 77–117). Newark, DE: International Reading Association.

Association for Middle Level Education. (2010). *This we believe. Keys to educating young adolescents.* Westerville, OH: Author.

Baumann, J. F. (2005). Vocabulary-comprehension relationships. In J. V. H. B. Maloch, D. L. Schallert, C. M. Fairbanks, & J. Worthy (Eds.), *54th yearbook of the National Reading Conference* (pp. 117–131). Oak Creek, WI: National Reading Conference.

Beck, I. L., McKeown, M. G., & Kucan, L. (2002). *Bringing words to life. Robust vocabulary instruction.* New York: Guilford Press.

Blachowicz, CL.Z, Baumann, J.E., Manyak, P.C. & Graves, M. (2014). Flood, fast, focus: Integrating vocabulary instruction in the classroom. In K. D. Wood, J. Paratore, B. Kissel & R. McCormack (Eds.), *What's new in literacy teaching? Weaving together time-honored practices with new research* (pp. 15–28). Newark, DE: International Reading Association.

Blanton, W. Pilonieta, P., & Wood, K. (2007). Promoting meaningful adolescent reading instruction through integrated literacy circles. In J. Lewis & G. Moorman (Eds.), *Adolescent literacy instruction. Policies and promising practices* (pp. 212–237). Newark, DE: International Reading Association.

Brown, D. F., & Knowles, T. (2007). *What every middle school teacher should know* (2nd ed.). Portsmouth, NH: Heinemann.

Collins, S. (2008). *The hunger games.* New York, NY: Scholastic.

Common Core State Standards Initiative. (2010). *Common Core State Standards for English language arts & literacy in history/social studies, science, and technical subjects.* Washington, DC. National Governors Association Center for Best Practices and the Council of Chief State School Officers.

Cummins, S. (2012). *Close reading of informational texts. Assessment driven instruction in grades 3–8.* New York: Guilford Press.

Daniels, H. (1994). *Literature circles: Voice and choice in the student–centered classroom.* Portland, ME: Stenhouse.

Daniels, H. (2002). Expository text in literary circles. *Voices from the Middle, 9*(4), 7–14.

Draper, R. J., Ed. (2012). *Re-imagining content area literacy instruction.* New York: Teachers College Press.

Dunston, P. & Gambrell, L. (2009). Motivating adolescent learners to read. In K. D. Wood and W. E. Blanton (Eds.), *Literacy instruction for adolescents. Research based practice* (pp.269–286). New York: Guilford Press.

Fisher, D. & Frey, N. (2012). *Improving adolescent literacy: Content area strategies at work* (3rd ed.). Boston, MA: Pearson.

Flood, J., Heath, S. B., & Lapp, D. (Eds.). (2007). *Handbook of research on teaching literacy through the communicative and visual arts, Volume II.* Newark, DE: International Reading Association.

Frey, N., & Fisher, D. (2006). *Language arts workshop. Purposeful reading and writing instruction* (1st ed.). Upper Saddle River, NJ: Prentice Hall.

Frey, N., & Fisher, D. (2012). *Common core English language arts in a PLC at work, grades 6–8.* Bloomington, IN: Solution Tree.

Gunning, T.G. (2012). *Reading success for all students. Using formative assessment to guide instruction and intervention.* San Francisco, CA: Jossey-Bass.

Guthrie, J. T. (Ed.). (2007). *Engaging adolescents in reading.* Thousand Oaks, CA: Corwin.

International Literacy Association. (2012). *Adolescent literacy instruction. A position paper of the International Reading Association.* Newark, DE: Author.

Lehman, B. (2007). *Children's literature and learning. Literary study across the curriculum.* New York: Teachers College Press.

Pearson, P. D., & Gallagher, M. C. (1983). The instruction of reading comprehension. *Contemporary Educational Psychology, 8*(3), 317–344.

RAND Reading Study Group. (2002). *Reading for understanding; Toward an R & D program in reading comprehension.* Santa Monica, CA: Science and Technology Policy Institute, Rand Education.

Samblis, K. (2006). Think tac toe. A motivating method of increasing comprehension. *The Reading Teacher, 59*(7), 691–694.

Tierney, R. J., & Readence, J. E. (2000). *Reading strategies and practices. A compendium* (5th ed.). Boston: Allyn & Bacon.

Tovani, C. (2004). *Do I really have to teach reading? Content comprehension grades 6–12.* Portland, ME: Stenhouse Publishers.

Vacca, R.T., Vacca, J.L., & Mraz, M.E. (2013). *Content area reading. Literacy and learning* (11th ed.). Saddle River, NJ: Pearson.

Wood, K. D. (2002). Aiding comprehension with the imagine, elaborate, predict and confirm (IEPC) strategy. *Middle School Journal, 33*(3), 47–54.

Wood, K. D. (2002). Differentiating reading and writing lessons to promote content learning. In C. C. Block, L. B Gambrell, & M. Pressley (Eds.), *Improving comprehension instruction. Rethinking research, theory, and classroom practice* (pp. 155–180). San Francisco, CA & Newark, DE: Jossey-Bass & International Reading Association.

Wood, K. D., Lapp, D., Flood, J., & Taylor, D. B. (2008). *Guiding readers through text. Strategy guides for new times* (2nd ed.). Newark, DE: International Reading Association.

Wood, K. D., Stover, K., Pilonieta, P., & Taylor, B. (2012). Don't skip the graphics! Focusing students' attention on the visual aids in digital and traditional texts. *Middle School Journal, 43*(4), 60–68.

Wood, K. D., Stover, K., & Taylor, D. B. (2015). *Smuggling writing in K–5 classrooms. Standards-based instruction for the 21st century learner.* Thousand Oaks, CA: Corwin.

Wood, K. D., Taylor, D. B., & Stover, K. (2015). *Smuggling writing in 6–12 classrooms. Standards-based instruction for the 21st century learner.* Thousand Oaks, CA: Corwin.

Yopp, R., & Yopp, H. (2007). 10 important words plus. *The Reading Teacher, 61,* 157–160.

Young, T. A., & Hadaway, N. L. (2006). *Supporting the literacy development of English learners. Increasing success in all classrooms.* Newark, DE: International Reading Association.

Zygouris-Coe, V., Wiggins, M. B., & Smith, L. H. (2004). Engaging students with text. The 3-2-1 strategy. *The Reading Teacher, 58,* 381–384.

Section II

What Are Best Practices for Vocabulary Instruction?

Middle grades students are faced with an increasing demand to increase vocabulary across all content-area disciplines. This increased demand in word knowledge has far-reaching implications as limited word knowledge directly influences students' ability to read and comprehend difficult content. The Common Core State Standards (CCSS) specify that students in the middle grades must be able to:

> Acquire and use accurately a range of general academic and domain-specific words and phrases sufficient for reading, writing, speaking, and listening at the college and career readiness level; demonstrate independence in gathering vocabulary knowledge when encountering an unknown term important to comprehension or expression (CCSS.ELA-Literacy.CCRA.L.6, 2010).

The CCSS place greater demands on middle grades students to acquire vocabulary and for teachers to teach vocabulary in meaningful ways. In truth, vocabulary knowledge is a basic component of comprehension. When students do not understand the meaning of words, they in turn cannot meet the demands in content-area classrooms. With this added pressure, classroom teachers often ask, ***How do I integrate vocabulary instruction in my discipline area?***

The term *vocabulary literacy* (Wood, 2009; Wood, Harmon & Taylor 2011) expands our thinking about word knowledge and word study beyond the surface, definitional level to the comprehension level. Vocabulary teaching and learning is not a task isolated from other dimensions of instruction. Rather, the act of promoting vocabulary literacy is multidimensional and involves making the connection between vocabulary and comprehension using all aspects of literacy: reading, writing, listening, speaking, viewing, and visually representing (Standards for the English Language Arts, 1996). When vocabulary is taught using a surface, definitional approach, students leave the experience with an inadequate understanding and no long-term retention of key terms. This linear approach to vocabulary instruction is depicted in Figure 1. Here, instruction begins from the bottom up—beginning at the word level and a corresponding definition, then attending to sentences and paragraphs, and ultimately focusing on comprehension as the final element.

Figure 1. *Linear Vocabulary Instruction Model*

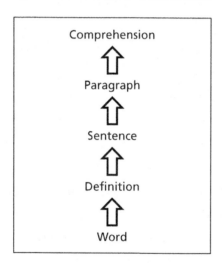

On the other hand, when vocabulary is taught using a comprehension-based vocabulary literacy approach, students process word meanings more deeply and actively engage in multimodal activities designed to promote strategic learning. This section illustrates vocabulary literacy and its close connection to comprehension, and then explains six instructional guidelines for integrating vocabulary literacy in content-area classrooms.

Vocabulary Literacy. Figure 2 identifies the features of vocabulary literacy. The circle outside "Target Words" emphasizes the importance of the reader, the text, and the activity in comprehension. The next concentric circle illustrates the important connection between vocabulary and comprehension using all aspects of literacy. reading, writing, listening, speaking, and viewing.

Figure 2. *Reader, Text, and Activity to Promote Vocabulary Literacy.*
RAND Reading Study Group 2002 Report "Reading for Understanding"

Six Guidelines for Promoting Vocabulary Literacy. Vocabulary

teaching and learning is not a task isolated from other dimensions of instruction. Rather, the act of promoting vocabulary literacy is crucial to comprehension, and vocabulary instruction in the content areas is essential for students to learn. Six guidelines that foster vocabulary development in the middle grades are giving students choice, moving beyond surface-level for deeper understandings of conceptually loaded terms, creating a print rich environment, encouraging collaboration and discussion, providing structured lessons, and underscoring text use of vocabulary. Based on research, the six guidelines have proven to be effective in the classroom (Brabham & Villaume (2002); Harmon, Wood, Hedrick, & Gress (2008); Graves, 2006; Ruddell & Shearer (2002); Vintinner, 2009).

Provide Students with Choices

Actively engaging students in decision making about which terms to learn at the middle level is developmentally appropriate because it is grounded in the reader's personal, motivational, experiential dimension. Typically this choice is left to the teacher or to the published textbook materials used in the classroom. In commercial texts, words are isolated and sometimes highlighted, often with limited instructional suggestions.

Personal Vocabulary Journal

Goal. Students choose vocabulary words that they will later share in peer discussions and/or see their value later as they appear on tests.

Benefits. Provides students the opportunity to identify new words, then to correctly use the new words acquired by studying their different relationships to other words. Figure 3 is an example of the template to serve as a procedural guideline for classroom teachers to implement the personal vocabulary journal. Figure 4 illustrates a sample lesson as a teacher would model.

Developmentally Appropriate. This strategy is grounded in the reader's personal, motivational, and experiential dimension and involves giving students a choice in deciding which words to learn.

Teacher Actions.

- Have students recall a time when they encountered a new word and wondered what it meant; tell them that they will select the important words (or some of them) for the upcoming unit.

- Create a blank vocabulary form and demonstrate how to select important vocabulary words by thinking aloud as you fill in a sample.

- Distribute copies of the personal vocabulary journal collection handout. Encourage students to record in it *any* word in any class that interests them—not necessarily ones related to the class topics. Explain how beneficial this action is.

Student Actions.

- Record on the blank vocabulary form one or two (or more) vocabulary terms of interest to them or relate to the current unit of study

- In groups of five to eight students share words from their vocabulary journals. Act out their words or make drawings to depict their meanings (display these drawings on your word wall).

Additional Options. Have students select two or three vocabulary words from their Personal Vocabulary Journals for weekly or unit vocabulary tests. Students can also choose two or three words from their journal to add to their word wall.

ELL Tip. Adapt the personal vocabulary journal for use with English language learners and second language learners. Have students write vocabulary words in both languages and include definitions and examples in both languages. Provide many opportunities for ELLs to hear the words, speak the words, see the words, and read the words. Using visuals, shared reading, games, and partner buddies will assist ELL learners.

Figure 3. *Personal Vocabulary Journal (Wood, 1994)*

My new word is	
It is related to	
I found it	
I think it means	
Definition	
Example	
Picture	

Figure 4. *Teacher Modeling a Personal Vocabulary Journal for Science*

Today, I am thinking about my new word...and the new word I have chosen is squall.

I chose squall because it is related to our science unit on weather but before I can understand how it relates to our reading, I need to know more about the word.

I think it means rainstorm, but just to be sure, I went to the weather station on TV to learn more about the word.

I think it means rain storm.

The appropriate dictionary definition is a sudden gust of wind; a black squall has dark clouds; a thick squall has hail or sleet.

Now, I can see how it relates to our reading. The specific context on how the word is used in our reading is New Yorkers were surprised by a thick squall early this morning. No precipitation is expected tomorrow, however.

My sentence is the black squall scared the young children as they played ball in the street.

Pick a Word—Not Just Any Word (Harmon, Wood, Hedrick, & Gress, 2008).

Goal. Collaborate with classmates to select important words related to the unit under study; produce group presentation to the class.

Developmentally Appropriate. The strategy meets students' social interaction needs as they practice collaborating with their peers. As they assert reasons for their choices, they develop their sense of identity and self-efficacy.

Benefits. Students increase word consciousness and gain interest in an important topic as they approach it from their viewpoint.

The strategy is a framework of four phases once the texts have been chosen and students are grouped.

Teacher Actions.

- Selects informational texts and Internet passages related to different aspects of the unit

- Divides the class into two large groups and gives each group one of the topics

- Divides each of the two large groups into two subgroups who read the same topic from different sources

- Conducts further rounds of dividing the class into two large groups and then into subgroups to cover more topics related to the unit.

Student Actions.

Phase 1. Individual Reading of the Text. Students read their assigned passage independently and code the text underlining important ideas and circling critical words and phrases. They list the circled words in a chart and provide a reason that the word is important to understanding the passage.

Phase 2. Same Text Small Groups. Students meet with other students who read the same passage comparing their lists of words. The groups decide which five to eight words to teach the class, noting the words that more than one group member chose. They list them in a chart and provide reasons the words are important.

Phase 3. Same Topic Large Groups. Students reading same topic meet as a large group and each subgroup selects a spokesperson to share words and information about its passage. The large group compares the words and information about the topic, noting overlapping and new information. The group prepares a teaching presentation as they list the words, the reasons for selecting the words, and the important information about the topic.

Phase 4. Teaching the Class Activities. Each group chooses to either (1) develop a digital visual presentation, or, (2) create a review game.

Teacher Actions.

- Continually assess students' work through the phases and each group's progress toward completing the tasks.

- Monitor the words chosen and encourage students to think deeply about the importance of the terms selected.

- Develop a checklist to serve as a guide for students and a rubric for students and the teacher to assess the final products that showcase the students' knowledge of the vocabulary words.

Example. *See Appendix F for an eighth grade Holocaust unit example of Pick a Word—Not Just Any Word, complete with student charts.*

Move Beyond Surface-level for Deeper Understanding

Students need to apply the meanings of newly introduced terms in a variety of activities that not only build vocabulary literacy but also impact comprehension. For vocabulary instruction in the content areas to be effective, instruction should move beyond a linear, definitional level to instruction that permits students to process terms in multiple, meaningful ways (Beck, McKeown, & Kucan, 2013; Graves, 2006). Successful vocabulary instruction must include vocabulary instruction that not only builds knowledge of vocabulary terms, but connects the meaning of these terms to the background knowledge of the learner (Taylor, Mraz, Nichols, Rickelman, & Wood, 2009). Moreover, students should be taught how to make connections between new word meanings and what they already know to create deep understanding of the vocabulary that can be applied in a variety of contexts (Taylor et al., 2009).

Think-Pair-Share. One simple but effective strategy is to pair students and allow them to Think-Pair-Share. Give students a vocabulary word to think about and allow them a few moments to think about the word (Lyman, 1987). Then have students share their thoughts with a partner and have them come to an agreement about what meaning of the word they will share with the class. A modification of this strategy adds a writing dimension, Think-Pair-Share (Wood, Stover & Taylor, in press) where students work in pairs to write a paragraph about their thinking about a topic. An extension of this, called Think-Pair-Share and Write (Wood, Stover, & Taylor, in press) is to allow students to work in pairs to write a paragraph using the word or concept.

Elicit Prior Knowledge. A second effective and simple strategy is to ask students higher-level questions related to vocabulary words to explore students' prior knowledge of vocabulary terms. For example, instead of asking students in a geometry class to engage in the low-level cognitive process of defining terms such as polygon, parallelogram, and rhombus, the teacher can ask probing questions at a higher cognitive level, such as: What distinguishing characteristic determines a polygon from a circle? What geometric shape can be more than one shape? Students must use what they know about the terms to formulate the correct response to each question.

Meaningful Questions and Prompts. Ensure that students have a clear understanding of the terms so they can transfer these understandings to other learning situations. If students are to move beyond a definitional level of word meaning, then students need sufficient time to study words. The research is clear that effective vocabulary instruction provides opportunities for students to learn the meaning of words in the context of study and to design instruction that allows students time to learn new words through multiple opportunities to apply word learning strategies (Graves, 2006).

List-Group-Label and Write. List-Group-Label and Write is a time-tested strategy that involves brainstorming words related to a particular topic or theme and then sorting those words into various categories (Taba, 1967; Wood, Stover & Taylor, 2015).

>   **Goal.** The goal is to build background knowledge related to a particular topic.

>   **Benefits.** Students build conceptual understanding of content-specific vocabulary words.

>   **Teacher Actions.** The teacher selects a topic or theme from the content to be studied.

>   **Student Actions.** Students work individually or in small groups to brainstorm the related topic presented by the teacher. The teacher may also contribute words to this list. Once words are brainstormed, students

group two or more words and list them together. They also create a label that defines or describes the categorization. Once words are categorized (grouped and labeled), new words can be added to each category. The students then discuss their rationale for organizing and grouping the words and, as an extension, work in pairs or small groups to compose a paragraph using the words in the categories (Wood, Stover, & Taylor, 2015).

Word Sorts. Word sort (Allen, 2007) activities are done in much the same way as List-Group-Label except the words and categories are usually predefined by the teacher.

Goal. To determine connections, patterns, and relationships among words.

Benefits. Word sorts are an effective strategy to activate prior knowledge and provide the schema for students to analyze the words by looking for similar patterns. Students develop a deeper understanding of what a word means from its basic level to connecting it with other words and concepts to convey a more sophisticated meaning in a context.

Teacher Actions. Depending on the specific content discipline, the teacher chooses the categories for the words.

Student Actions. Students work individually or in small groups to sort the words in the predetermined categories. Once words are sorted, the students then discuss their rationale for organizing and grouping the words.

Develop Vocabulary Awareness Through a Print-rich Environment

An important aspect of a strong vocabulary program is to engage students in learning new words. As teachers, we need to develop word consciousness within our students and maintain their interest in words. Students not only learn words through direct instruction, but they also develop their knowledge and exposure to new words indirectly through independent reading, word walls, and exposure to print across the school day. The optimal goal for middle grades classroom teachers is to build word consciousness (Blachowicz & Fisher, 2014). Print-rich environments include classroom libraries, objects labeled throughout the room, posters, maps, multimedia centers, newsprint, bulletin boards, and student-produced writing and art.

Interactive Word Wall. Another feature common in a print-rich environment is the interactive word wall, which involves extensive teacher modeling and consistent dialogue as students make connections to key terms by assigning each of them a color, a symbol, and a context. In conjunction, the interactive word wall builds on the various dimensions of literacy (reading, writing, speaking, listening, viewing, and visually representing) to promote content area learning.

To use an interactive word wall, the process is (a) selecting words to teach, (b) introducing words, (c) making connections to the words, (d) using the words in meaningful ways, and (e) sharing the word meanings. These steps can be applied to vocabulary instruction in any content area.

a. **Select the Words.** Select conceptually important words from a passage about the topic. Target for direct instruction only a few of the most critical terms from all of those unfamiliar to some students. For example, in a social studies passage about the U.S. in the 1950s and the 1960s, the teacher may decide that the following terms are important for comprehension. *Sputnik, invincible, devastating, prestige, communism, dominated, arsenal, nuclear annihilation, National Defense Education Act of 1958,* and *mediocre.*

b. **Introduce and Model the Lesson.** Introduce the terms using a rich content area context that enables students to form a reasonable meaning for the term. The teacher typically writes this because naturally occurring contexts containing unfamiliar terms may not be very helpful to students. For example, a teacher could use the following instructional context for the word *invincible.*

> After defeating Germany and the Axis powers during World War II in the 1940s, the United States became an even stronger and more powerful country. In the 1950s the American people felt that no country could ever match their strength and power. However, they no longer felt *invincible* after the Soviet Union launched the first unmanned satellite into space in 1957.

From such a paragraph, the teacher and students construct a student-friendly definition for *invincible.* For example, instead of the dictionary definition "incapable of being conquered, defeated, or subdued" (from www.dictionary.com), a more understandable definition would be "describes how you feel when you think that no one person or no one thing can beat you or take you down or win you over."

Instructional Context. While *communism* is on the decline today, some countries, such as Cuba, China, and North Korea, still try to maintain the social order in which the political party dominates the country, and the goods and services are shared by the people, with title personal ownership for anyone.

c. **Make Connections with the Terms.** After students have a clear understanding of the word meanings, they engage in word wall activities for making connections, including assigning a color to the word meanings, drawing a symbol, and illustrating a situation. For these tasks, the teacher divides the class into small groups comprised of three or four students. Each group is assigned two of the targeted words.

Connections to Color. Students write each term on a flash card and then decide on a color that might be representative of the word's meaning. Any color can be matched to a word, as long as the student can provide a reasonable justification tied to the word's meaning. Once the student groups have agreed on the colors for the words, they color each flash card with the designated color and then hang the card on the word wall.

Connections to Symbols. Groups draw a symbol on an index card to represent the term. Students decide on a symbol that will trigger recollection of the word's meaning. The symbols are then placed to the left of the flash card of the corresponding word on the word wall (see examples in Figures 1 & 2).

Connections to Contexts. Students think of situations or contexts in which the term can be used and to illustrate the situation or context on another index card. For example, for the word *invincible*, one context for using this term could be in reference to an *invincible* army attacking enemies. For each of these examples, students draw simple illustrations as reminders of contexts to associate with the terms. The students place the index card illustrating a situation associated with the word to the right of the flash card on the word wall.

d. **Use the Words in Meaningful Ways.** Student groups use the word meanings to develop meaningful prompts and questions. Using strategies developed by Beck, McKeown, and Kucan (2013), the teacher models meaning prompts, sentence completions, and word associations for the students. Here are a few examples with our targeted words.

e. **Share the New Learning.** Students synthesize what they have learned. Gathering together all of the information they have about their assigned terms, groups create a class presentation. Their task is to become the teacher to help other classmates extend and reinforce understanding of the words. Students should include the instructional contexts: clearly understandable definitions; references to and explanations of the colors, symbols, and situations of the words on the word wall; and interactive discussions whereby the classmates provide responses to the meaningful prompts, sentence completions, and word associations.

Encourage Collaboration and Discussion

Student collaboration and discussion can make learning new concepts and vocabulary more active, engaging, and comprehension-based, in contrast to traditional linear approaches to teaching vocabulary that are less effective and often involve simply defining the target words. While collaborating and discussing, students use words in new contexts and in novel ways.

Literature Circles. Using both fiction and nonfiction, literature circles can highlight vocabulary and encourage discussion (Daniels, 2002). Daniels defines literature circles as a small, temporary reading group in which each member undertakes certain responsibilities during discussion time. The students meet regularly, and the roles or responsibilities rotate at the conclusion of each session or meeting. The typical procedure for implementation involves the teacher presenting the text through a book talk. Students choose numbers by ballot, numbering one through four, and the teacher forms the groups and disperses the books. The groups decide how much each member can read before they next meet and each member is allocated a role. Students then complete their reading individually and prepare for their literature circle discussion. Discussion takes place within the literature circle. At the end, the group decides how much each member can read before they next meet. Each member is allocated a new role.

The roles include the *Discussion Director,* the student who leads the group by preparing a brief summary of the pages read and then devises questions to provoke meaningful thought and discussion; the *Literary Illuminator,* the student who identifies a controversial or a provocative passage to share with the group; the *Creative Connector,* the participant who finds a way to link the reading to his or her own life experiences; and the *Wordsmith,* the group member who selects a few words to share with other group members and plans an activity to teach the words.

Word Wizard.

Goal. While working in circles and groups, the student responsible for the "word wizard" role examines the text carefully for words that are interesting, unfamiliar, and especially important for readers to understand.

Benefits. The role allows students to talk, question, connect, and think more deeply about how the words' meanings impact their understanding of the passage.

Student Actions. The words a writer chooses are an important ingredient of the author's craft. The word wizard's job is to be on the lookout for a few words that have special meaning in the assigned reading selection. The student:

- Jots down puzzling or unfamiliar words while reading. Later, the student looks up the definitions in either a dictionary or some other source.

- Notes words that stand out somehow in the reading—words that are repeated a lot, used in an unusual way, or are crucial to the meaning of the text. The student shares with the group information about usage of the words.

Note. When discussing vocabulary, students should always refer to the text to examine the word in context.

Digital Tools. Collaborative discussions for vocabulary teaching and learning are increasingly supported through digital tools. For example, students can use Voice Thread (http.//voicethread.com) to discuss, pose multiple definitions, and provide real-world examples using images and text. This web-based program allows students to comment on images or texts using audio, video, text, or file uploads. Teachers and students can upload selections of text, images, and key vocabulary, and can conduct an online asynchronous discussion using one of the five formats listed above.

Provide a Structured Lesson Framework

P.E.A.R. instructional Framework (Harmon & Wood, 2008)

Goal. Provides a structure for teaching vocabulary within a content lesson using four steps: Preparation, Explanation, Application, and Reinforcement.

Benefits. The strategy is ideal for students who need structure. Within the framework are formative and summative assessment opportunities as well as opportunities for students to evaluate their own knowledge.

Teacher Actions.

Preparation. The teacher selects important words and phrases, limiting the number so as not to overwhelm students. These words should be the most critical to understanding the concepts in the passage or learning session. This step can include assessment of prior knowledge using a tool such as the *knowledge rating scale* (Blachowicz & Fisher, 2006) shown in Figure 5 for geography terms. The activity enables students to determine their own knowledge about the terms and also serves as a summative assessment to help students evaluate their own learning.

Figure 5. *Knowledge Rating Scale*

Word	I know this word. It means...	The word looks familiar.	I do not know this word.	New in-formation from the text.
global warming				
urbanization				
urban sprawl				
megalopolis				
textiles				

Explanation. Once teachers have selected the vocabulary, the next step is to introduce the words and terms to the students using clearly understandable definitions—what Beck and her colleagues call student-friendly definitions (Beck, McKeown, & Kucan, 2013). For example, for the term *urban sprawl,* instead of the definition "the unplanned, uncontrolled spreading of urban development into areas adjoining the edge of a city," a more easily understood definition could be "a word that describes what happens when a city starts spreading farther and farther out into the area around it." These student-friendly definitions also need to be accompanied by supportive instructional contexts (Graves, 2006). In this case, the teacher can show students various photographs that depict *urban sprawl.* Next, the teacher introduces key terms using student-friendly definitions and non-textbook explanations with phrases familiar to students. The teacher also provides additional support materials further illustrating a concept, such as pictures, streaming video, and virtual tours.

Student Actions.

> **Application.** After an interactive discussion of the chosen terms, students move beyond the surface definition to a deeper understanding and apply the words and terms in meaningful activities. The application step can be accomplished through variations of teacher-prompted activities, such as the following suggestions recommended by Beck, McKeown, and Kucan (2013).
>
> - Meaningful-use prompts
> - Things you would expect to see in an **urbanized** area.
>   - Examples of textiles.
>
> - Statement completions
>   - **Urbanization** creates major changes in the landscape of an area because…
>   - **Urbanization** may be contributing to **global warming** because…
>
> - Word associations
>   - Which word is used when talking about renovating old warehouses in inner cities?
>   - Which word would you use when talking about buying and selling goods from other countries?
>
> - Meaningful questions
> - Would you expect to find **textile** mills in a **megalopolis**?
>   - Would **urban** sprawl have an impact on the **Dairy Belt**?

If we only ask students to provide definitions for terms, then they can memorize definitions, pass the tests, and not really have an understanding of the concepts. However, questions and prompts such as those above require that students apply what they know about the terms in order to successfully answer them. Such responses are more indicative of learning.

Reinforcement. Because students need multiple encounters with key words to solidify their understanding, the final phase of P.E.A.R. involves emphasis, synthesis, and a review of the terms in a different context. Numerous strategies can be used for this purpose, such as cubing, in which students discuss a term from different dimensions including describing, comparing and contrasting, associating, analyzing, applying, and arguing (see Figure 6).

Figure 6. *Cubing (Bean, Readence, & Baldwin, 2008)*

TERM: MARKET ECONOMY	
Describe it.	Compare or contrast it.
A market economy is one type of economic system. An economic system is the way in which a country manages its money, materials, and labor.	*A market economy is similar to capitalism and free enterprise.*
A market economy allows the people to freely choose what to buy and sell.	*A market economy is different from a planned or command economy in which the government decides what to buy and sell and at what price.*
Associate it.	Analyze it.
I think a market economy allows people the opportunity to earn more money by opening their own businesses.	*There is competition in a market economy, and this can keep prices down.*
	The producers of goods and services listen to the wants and needs of the consumers.
Apply it.	Argue for or against it.
Every time I go shopping for a new video game, I can be grateful for the market economy in America. If it wouldn't be for this type of economy, I think the selection of games would not be as wide as it is at the stores.	*I support a market economy. It gives me many choices when I am looking for things, and it gives me the opportunity to open my own business if I like.*

Another example is the R.A.F.T. activity in Figure 7 (Santa, Haven, & Harrison, 2008). R.A.F.T. stands for *role, audience, form,* and *topic.* Students select one of the tasks to write about, and they use newly learned vocabulary in the writing.

Figure 7. *RAFT World Geography Example*

ROLE	AUDIENCE	FORMAT	TOPIC
Naturalist John Muir	Lumber industry	Commercial	Conservation of natural resources
Meteorologist	People along the Texas Gulf Coast	Broadcast script for television	Approaching category 4 hurricane
Salmon	Grand Coulee Dam	Brochure	Difficulties caused by the dam
Director of the National Park Service	Outdoor enthusiasts	Page in a guidebook	3 most popular hiking trails in the United States
Tour director	People who like to go on tours	Internet website	7-day tour of western Canada
Lewis of Lewis and Clark	President Thomas Jefferson	Letter	Request for more money to continue the expedition to the south
Mountain climber climbing Mt. Everest	Himself or herself	Poem	Experience of climbing the mountain

Teach Text Structures and Features

The increasingly complex and sophisticated texts used in middle and secondary level content classrooms are challenging to many students as they build and expand their knowledge bases across the different disciplines. Each content area has unique language structures and specialized vocabulary for conveying and communicating knowledge (Fang & Schleppegrell, 2008). Moreover, since the texts in these disciplines contain both external and internal features that can influence the way in which vocabulary and comprehension intersect, it is important to show students how these features work. In regard to external features, publishers highlight critical terminology in **bold print**, sometimes offer definitions in a sidebar, and typically include a glossary at the end of the text. In addition, publishers may include illustrations of important vocabulary terms. For electronic texts, hyperlinks enable students to find meanings of unfamiliar words with one mouse click. These hyperlinks can lead to written texts of word meanings or provide multimedia sources to explain vocabulary. Such features in both traditional and electronic texts provide critical vocabulary support that, in turn, aids in comprehension. Teachers can model their thinking as they encounter these external features in texts, articulating how the features make them attend to the meanings of the words being highlighted. Such modeling can strengthen students' metacognitive awareness of how to effectively use these features.

Internal text structures involve the ways in which authors themselves use language and words to craft their ideas. It is important for students to know the five most commonly used internal text structures.

Description. Sensory and descriptive details help readers visualize information. It shares the who, what, where, when, why, and how of a topic/subject.

Sequence & Order.

> ***Sequence of Events.*** Chronological texts present events in a sequence from beginning to end.

> ***How-To.*** How-To texts organize the information in a series of directions.

Compare & Contrast. Authors use comparisons to describe ideas to readers. Similarities and differences are shared.

Cause & Effect. Informational texts often describe cause and effect relationships. The text describes events and identifies reasons (causes) for why the event happened.

Problem & Solution. The text introduces and describes a problem and presents one or more solutions.

Summary

When teachers use a linear, bottom-up approach to vocabulary instruction, students are not required to process word meanings and often do not recall words beyond their first experience. The term *vocabulary literacy* (Wood, 2009; Wood, Harmon & Taylor, 2011) highlights the need for a broader view of vocabulary development, a comprehension-based view of word study that never loses sight of the connection to understanding. The strategies in this chapter approach word study metacognitively and broadly to move beyond the word level and take into consideration the reader, the text, the activity, and all strands of literacy: reading, writing, listening, speaking, and viewing.

Acknowledgements

Harmon, J. M., Wood, K. D., Hedrick, W. B., & Gress, M. (2008). "Pick a word—not just any word". Using vocabulary self-selection with expository texts. *Middle School Journal, 40*(1), 43–52.

Harmon, J. M., Wood, K. D., Kiser, K. (2009). Promoting vocabulary learning with the interactive word wall. *Middle School Journal, 40(3),* 58–63.

Nichols, W. D., Rupley, W. H., Blair, T. R., & Wood, K. D. (2008). Vocabulary strategies for linguistically diverse learners. *Middle School Journal, 39*(3), 65–69.

Wood, K. D. & Tinajero, J. (2002). Using pictures to teach content to second language learners. *Middle School Journal, 33*(5), 47–51.

Wood, K. D., Harmon, J. M., & Taylor, B. (2011). Guidelines for integrating comprehension-based word study in content classrooms. *Middle School Journal, 42*(5), 57–64.

References

Allen, J. (2007). *Inside words. Tools for teaching academic vocabulary, grades 4–12.* Portland, ME: Stenhouse.

Bean, T. W., Readence, J. E., & Baldwin, R. S. (2008). *Content area literacy. An integrated approach* (9th ed.). Dubuque, IA: Kendall Hunt.

Blachowicz, C., & Fisher, P. J. (2006). *Teaching vocabulary in all classrooms* (3rd ed.). Upper Saddle River, NJ: Pearson Education.

Brabham E. G., & Villaume, S. K. (2002). Vocabulary instructions. Concerns and visions. *The Reading Teacher, 56,* 264–268.

Blachowicz, C. & Fisher, P. (2014). *Teaching vocabulary in all classrooms.* Boston: Pearson.

Common Core State Standards Initiative. (2010). *Common Core Standards for English language arts & literacy in history, social studies, science, and technical subjects.* Washington, DC. National Governors Association Center for Best Practices and the Council of Chief State School Officers.

Cordova, D. I., & Lepper, M. R. (1996). Intrinsic motivation and the process of learning. Beneficial effects of contextualization, personalization and choice. *Journal of Educational Psychology, 88,* 715–730.

Cunningham, P. M. (2000). *Phonics they use. Words for reading and writing.* New York: Longman.

Daniels, H. (2002). *Literature circles. Voice and choice in book clubs and reading groups.* Portland, ME: Stenhouse.

Fang, Z., & Schleppegrell, M. J. (2008). *Reading in secondary content areas. A language-based pedagogy.* Ann Arbor, MI: The University of Michigan Press.

Fisher, P. J., Blachowicz, C. L. Z., & Smith, J. C. (1991). Vocabulary learning in literature discussion groups. In J. Zutell & S. McCormick (Eds.), *Learner factors/teacher factors. Issues in literacy research and instruction* (pp.201–209). Chicago: National Reading Conference.

Graves, M. F. (2006). *The vocabulary book. Learning and instruction.* Newark, DE: International Reading Association.

Harmon, J. M., Hedrick, W. B., & Wood, K. D. (2005). Research on vocabulary instruction in the content areas. Implications for struggling readers. *Reading and Writing Quarterly, 21,* 261–280.

Harmon, J., & Wood, K. (2008, October). Content area vocabulary. A critical key to conceptual learning. AdLIT In Perspective, Retrieved from http://ohiorc.org/adlit/inperspective/issue/2008-10/Article/feature.aspx

Harmon, J. M., Wood, K. D., Hedrick, W., & Gress, M. (2008). Pick a word—not just any word. Using vocabulary self-selection with expository texts. *Middle School Journal, 40*(1), 43 –51.

National Council of Teachers of English. (1996). *Standards for the English Language Arts.* Urbana, IL: Author.

Ruddell, M. R., & Shearer, B. A. (2002). "Extraordinary," "tremendous," "exhilarating," "magnificent". Middle school at-risk students become avid word learners with the Vocabulary Self-Collection Strategy (VSCS). *Journal of Adolescent and Adult Literacy, 45,* 352–353.

Taba, H. (1967). *Curriculum development; Theory and practice.* San Diego, CA: Harcourt College Publishers.

Taylor, B. D., Mraz, M., Nichols, W. D., Rickelman, R. J., & Wood, K. (2009). Using explicit instruction to promote vocabulary learning for struggling readers. *Reading and Writing Quarterly, 25*(2), 205–220.

Vintinner, J. P. (2009, November). A content analysis of vocabulary instruction in high school commercial literacy programs. Research presented at the 2009 annual conference of the Association of Literary Educators and Researchers, Charlotte, North Carolina.

Wood, K.D. (1994). *Practical strategies for improving instruction.* Columbus, OH: National Middle School Association.

Wood, K. D. (2009). *The case for improving adolescent literacy instruction. Rationale, research, recommendations.* Presentation for the International Reading Association, Phoenix, AZ.

Wood, K. D., & Harmon, J. M. (2008). The absolutes of vocabulary instruction. *Middle Ground, 12(1),* 29–31.

Wood, K. D., Stover, K., & Taylor, D. B. (2015). *Smuggling writing in K–5 classrooms. Standards-based instruction for the 21st century learner.* Thousand Oaks, CA: Corwin.

Wood, K. D., & Taylor, D. B. (2006). *Literacy strategies across the subject areas* (2nd ed.). New York: Allyn & Bacon.

Wood, K. D., Taylor, D. B., & Stover, K. (2015). *Smuggling writing in 6–12 classrooms. Standards-based instruction for the 21st century learner.* Thousand Oaks, CA: Corwin.

References for Holocaust unit

Cordova, D. I., & Lepper, M. R. (1996). Intrinsic motivation and the process of learning. Beneficial effects of contextualization, personalization, and choice. *Journal of Educational Psychology, 88,* 715–730.

Gambrell, L. B., & Marinak, B. A. (1997). Incentives and intrinsic motivation to read. In J.T. Guthrie & A. Wigfield (Eds.), *Reading engagement. Motivating reading through integrated instruction* (pp. 205–217). Newark, DE: International Reading Association.

Kohn, A. (1993). Choices for children. Why and how to let students decide. *Phi Delta Kappan, 75,* 8–16, 18–21.

Reynolds, P. L., & Symons, S. (2001). Motivational variables and children's text search. *Journal of Educational Psychology, 93,* 14–22.

Schraw, G., Flowerday, T., & Reisetter, M. F. (1998). The role of choice in reader engagement. *Journal of Educational Psychology, 90,* 705–714. Cambridge, MA: The Massachusetts Institute of Technology. (Original work published 1934)

References (Word Wall)

Beck, I. L., McKeown, M. G., & Kucan, L. (2013). *Bringing words to life. Robust vocabulary instruction* (2nd ed.). New York: Guilford Press.

Gambrell, L. B., & B. Marinak. (1997). Incentive and intrinsic motivation to read. In J.T. Guthrie & A. Wigfield (Eds.), *Reading engagement. Motivating readers through integrated instruction* (pp. 205–217). Newark, DE: International Reading Association.

Kohn, A. (1993). Choices for children. Why and how to let students decide. *Phi Delta Kappan,* 8–20.

Schatz, E. K., & Baldwin, R. S. (1986). Context clues are unreliable predictors of word meanings. *Reading Research Quarterly, 21,* 439–453.

Section III.

How Do I Integrate Writing?

For decades, research (Graham & Perin, 2007) has delivered the consistent message that our nation's children are writing infrequently, and consequently, not very proficiently. All too often, students spend a great deal of their school day with pencil in hand—typically engaged in short answer and fill-in the-blank exercises with little opportunity to actually compose a written passage of text.

Aware of this serious academic deficit, writers of the Common Core State Standards (Common Core State Standards Initiative, 2010) have called for an increased emphasis on writing for middle level literacy in history/social studies, science, and the technical subjects. Writing formats include arguments, expository/informational pieces, and narratives (Council of Chief State School Officers, 2010). As a result, teachers are now required to add writing instruction to their increasing list of responsibilities, and many are wondering.
How can I integrate writing in my discipline area?

To middle grades teachers who often teach more than 150 students a day, the thought of having yet another subject to teach is formidable. When viewed as a separate subject to teach—especially for a science teacher who may not have a language arts background—writing instruction can seem like an insurmountable burden. However, when viewed as a means of teaching subject matter, the task is far less threatening and often enjoyable for both teachers and students.

This section provides effective strategies for energizing writing in the content areas. The only way students will improve their writing skill is to practice writing as much as possible. In fact, we recommend that students write every day. Many of these efforts need not be graded in the formal sense or edited to perfection. They are practice writing sessions, and they can be integrated in all areas of the curriculum. In the least formal sense, the practice writing should be proofread by at least the writer and preferably by a classmate as well. Sometimes just reading aloud to oneself or a partner to determine "soundness"—how it sounds when spoken orally—is enough to catch a few errors in the composition. Next on the continuum would be editing in small groups with roles and areas of emphasis assigned to each group member, for example, punctuation, grammar, spelling, content, etc.

Communal Writing

Description. In this strategy, small groups of students put their heads together to develop a single composition.

Goal. Help students become better writers by practicing the process of writing.

Benefits. Communal writing is based on the extensive research on collaborative learning that has been found to positively affect everything from self-esteem to peer and race relationships (Wood, 1987; Wolsey, Wood, & Lapp, 2014). Teachers will find communal writing accomplishes many tasks. it enhances vocabulary development, provides writing practice, and serves as a means to synthesize content. Most importantly, middle grades students will be able to join the "writing community" with minimal risk and maximal opportunity for learning. Because there is one product per group, the strategy eliminates the "I can't get started because I don't know what to write" problem. The strategy focuses the writer who writes pages of disconnected, detailed content.

Developmentally Appropriate. "As young adolescents grow toward adulthood and develop their sense of identity, they are intensely interested and motivated to relate to those around them. Their identity formation is inextricably interwoven with their social, personal, and moral development" (Strahan, L'Esperance, Van Hoose, 2009, p. 62).

Teacher Actions. Pre-assign students to groups of four or five with each group becoming a "community of writers." By establishing writing groups in advance, the teacher can ensure a heterogeneous grouping arrangement in which students are able to assist fellow students.

It is important to specify the tasks each member of the group may be expected to undertake at the onset, and periodically rotate these roles. Suggested role descriptions for communal writing are:

- Contributor. All group members contribute ideas related to the topic.

- Recorder. An individual records the ideas suggested (in both rough and final draft stages).

- Reader. An individual reads aloud the composition for the group to assess "soundness" (in both rough and final draft stages).

- Proofreader. Group members (select one member or all) proofread the composition for punctuation, grammar, content, spelling, etc.

- Editor. Group-selected individual gives final stamp of approval to composition.

Student Actions. As with any community, students work together to contribute their individual strengths to the process, which may involve spelling, content knowledge, proofreading, or composing, to name a few. Students can earn grades as individuals for their cooperation in the tasks or for the group as a whole for completing the project.

Adaptations. Although a peer editing phase is an option, the teacher may decide to engage in communal writing solely for its value as either a prereading or background-building strategy or as a postreading or synthesizing strategy. As such, no formal editing needs to take place. However, it is recommended that communal writing, for the most part, be viewed as a means to provide writing practice for students, in which case, the assignment of a grade would not be necessary.

Story Impressions

Description. The story impressions strategy developed by McGinley and Denner (1987) has survived the test of time and has been modified (Wood & Taylor, 2006) and adapted to the digital age with alternative applications (Wood, Stover & Taylor, 2015). With the digital tool, https://bubbl.us, brainstorming is made easy and engaging for adolescent learners because of the online, interactive dimension. The teacher can create the template and students can complete the lesson online using the website. Whether online or in traditional format, the story impressions strategy requires that readers predict a story line using sequentially presented key words or phrases derived from the selection.

Goal. Leverage the importance of prediction to increasing students' understanding; bring all students' prior experiences to bear as they make reasonable guesses about what will occur; students create richer mental images and elaborations, which in turn, help them understand new concepts.

Benefits. The strategy can be used in content areas to elicit prior knowledge before reading the text; it addresses the integration of reading, writing, and vocabulary development while addressing the content area topic of study. It allows for students to create their impressions of what the actual topic of study will be through the use of multiple sources such as newspapers, trade books, online journal articles, etc.

Teacher Actions.

1. Explain to the students that very often it is possible to make reasonable predictions about something with a minimal amount of information. For example, show a portion of a familiar object or picture and have students guess the whole. Then relate this to reading

by telling students that previewing the title of a chapter, pictures, boldface print, and subheadings beforehand helps readers develop a mental set for the content to be studied.

2. Next, introduce the key words and phrases on the board or by giving each student or group a printed copy (Figure 1). Read through the words with the students and ask them to begin developing their impressions of what the story may be about. For modeling purposes, you may want to "talk through" a short example initially with the class as a whole before breaking them into small groups.

3. Pre-assign students to writing groups of four or five and allow them to move their desks in a composing circle, if possible. Tell them that they will work together to predict a story line based on some clue words. Give them a list of ordered concepts that will lead them to predict a story line as close to the actual selection as possible.

4. As the groups share their work later, point out how varied, and yet equally acceptable, the responses can be. Assure students that closeness of match with the author's story is not that important.

Student Actions. After reading the key phrases, readers develop an impression or anticipatory set. Then, they construct their predicted passage and use this as a blueprint or model to be confirmed or modified as they encounter the new information in the actual story. Groups read their story impressions to the class. Students then read the original selection and make comparisons. In their groups, students can read portions of the story and then retell the information to group members. Afterwards, or the next day, the groups or the class as a whole use the key words to retell the events of the actual selection.

Figure 1. *Story Impressions*

STORY IMPRESSIONS
Language Arts
"The Fog Horn" by Ray Bradbury

Sequentially ordered terms.

fog light	fog horn calls	waiting
McDunn	swimming	rushing
Tower	immense eyes	crashed
Nervously	subterranean	rescuers
Ascended	roared	gone
Something comes	isolation	deeps
Lighthouse	surface	

Students' predicted passage.

It was time to turn on the *fog light. McDunn* climbed the *tower nervously.* As he *ascended,* he thought about the legend that *something comes* to the *lighthouse* when the *fog horn calls* in the night.

The fog horn sounded and McDunn looked out. He saw something *swimming* toward him. What could it be? He could see *immense eyes* in a gigantic head! Was it some kind of *subterranean* monster? Just then something *roared.* Was it the monster or the wind? McDunn felt his *isolation* as he looked out over the *surface* of the water, *waiting* to see or hear something in the thick fog.

Suddenly, a large dark shape came rushing out of the fog and crashed into the rocks on the beach. It was a fishing boat. When the *rescuers* found the boat crew they were not hurt, but they acted very strange. They kept saying something about a sea monster chasing their boat. But if there ever was a monster, it was *gone* now—back to the *deeps.* Would it return? McDunn was sure it would.

Exchange-Compare Writing

Description. While the story impressions strategy is most appropriate for narrative material, this strategy is best used with expository material. This strategy can also be used online with such digital applications as Google Drive or Titan Pad (Wolsey, Wood & Lapp, 2014).

Benefits. Because students engage in this strategy in small groups, they are able to assist one another in contributing content and in the editing process. The strategy is multi-dimensional in that it covers key vocabulary and concepts in a selection, and involves prediction writing and comprehension within a single lesson.

Teacher Actions. The teacher gives students a list of approximately 10 to 15 key vocabulary terms. However, unlike the story impressions strategy, the key concepts here are introduced in random order. Alphabetizing the list is one way to emphasize that students can use the words in any order. Discuss unknown words in a meaningful context, asking students for elaborations. Group students in fours and fives heterogeneously.

Student Actions. Students use the words to develop a passage, predicting the actual selection. Students may use a dictionary to look up unknown words and select an appropriate definition. The groups can then read their predicted compositions to the remainder of the class, discussing the differences and similarities. Then, they, in effect, "exchange" their predicted passage for the actual passage by making comparisons and reacting to the selection from which the words were taken (see Figure 2).

EXCHANGE-COMPARE STRATEGY
Social Studies
"Governments and Economic Systems"

Selected words.

capitalism	production
communism	profit
competition	resources
economics	revolution
industry	socialism

Predicted passage.

The *economics* of the United States is based on *capitalism.* Natural *resources* are used for the *production* of goods. Then these goods are sold for a *profit.* Anyone can start an *industry* or a business to sell things. Businesses are in *competition* with each other. Some countries have *communism* or *socialism.* In Russia there was a *revolution* to make communism the form of government.

Capsule Vocabulary

Description. Unlike the previous two strategies, capsule vocabulary (Crist, 1975) is used after the reading or studying of content. Research shows that the mere process of targeting new words increases the likelihood that students will learn them from the context.

Goal. Target new vocabulary so students can focus on them while reading and learn definitions from context; using vocabulary in a new way (informally, in conversation, with partners rather than learning vocabulary list by memorizing) moves them beyond rigid memorization tasks to a higher level of understanding.

Teacher Actions.

1. Select, display, and review 10 to 15 target vocabulary terms (see Figure 3). Introduce the words in the pre-reading phase and instruct students to focus on them while reading, using the context to infer their meanings.

2. With the aid of the class, review each term using it informally in conversation to expand its meaning (Step 2 of Figure 3). The explanations serve as a model for the next step.

Student Actions.

1. Students work in pairs to use the vocabulary as a springboard for a conversation with their partners, checking off the terms as they are mentioned.

2. Students work in fours and fives to use as many of the target vocabulary as possible in the construction of a passage. Both Steps 1 and 2 can be timed, approximately 10 minutes each, to further expedite the process. By this time, the students have had numerous encounters with the significant vocabulary and concepts of the selection to help solidify their understanding and improve their retention.

Figure 3. *Capsule Vocabulary*

CAPSULE VOCABULARY
Science
"Arthropods"

Step 1. Present vocabulary

arthropods
exoskeleton
crustaceans
gills
segments
centipedes

millipedes
carnivorous
arachnids
prey
venom

Step 2. Review definitions

Teacher. *Animals with exoskeletons, such as crabs, do not have bones. Another name for an exoskeleton is what, class?*

Students. *Armor, or a hard, rigid covering.*

Teacher. *In literature, we might use metaphorical or exaggerated language to say that the soldier displayed an exoskeleton of steel when interrogated by his captors. Describe the soldier's behavior and appearance.*

Step 3. In pairs, students engage in conversational dialogue.

Student A. *I guess... all arthropods have an armor called exoskeletons, don't they?*

Student B. *That's right, and jointed legs. And some, like crustaceans, breathe through gills.*

Student A. *A turtle's shell is like an exoskeleton.*

Step 4. Partners work together to compose a paper on topic of arthropods.

Arthropods are invertebrate animals that have *exoskeletons* and jointed legs. There are more kinds of arthropods than all other animal species put together. Some types of arthropods are *crustaceans, centipedes,* and *millipedes, arachnids,* and insects.

Crabs and lobsters are crustaceans. They breathe through *gills* and their bodies are divided into *segments.* Centipedes and millipedes look like worms with legs. The difference between them is the number of legs on each segment. Also, centipedes are *carnivorous* and use poison to kill their food.

The name for arachnids carne from a Greek myth about a woman named Arachne. Their bodies are divided into two main sections and they have eight legs. Spiders and scorpions are arachnids. They both kill their *prey* with *venom.* Ticks are also arachnids. They don't have venom but they can spread diseases.

Story and Paragraph Frames

Description. Story frames are a sequence of spaces connected by key language elements. For narrative text, story frames help students identify the author's purpose or plot. Additionally, story frames are an excellent method to analyze a story's character. They can also be used as a means to guide and scaffold the language learning of students for whom English is a second language or are struggling with print (Amendum, 2015)

Goal. Provide practice for process of putting their thoughts into print; ease them into getting started and staying focused

Benefits. The use of story or paragraph frames is beneficial for a number of reasons: (1) they promote and channel peer interaction in a productive manner, (2) they help students who lack in writing proficiency to focus their ideas, (3) they provide a means for subject area teachers to incorporate writing practice with their instructional lesson, and (4) they make the task of writing more manageable for both the teacher and the students.

Developmentally Appropriate. Engages them; eases frustration with mechanical elements of writing; supports those students needing structure, those easily distracted, struggling students

Teacher Actions

1. **Modeling Stage.** As with any new strategy or concept, teachers should model frames before students use them individually. This may entail a number of modeling sessions with teachers applying one type of frame to several different selections.

    Teacher Actions. Explain the process of the lesson to the entire class to help students organize their thoughts into a logical written form. Display the frame before reading (or listening) to the story using an interactive white board.

Student Actions. Students read (or listen) to a sample selection with the framework in mind, which provides them with a purpose for reading (or listening). With teacher guidance, they fill in each line of the frame. Students reach a consensus on the information to be included. A volunteer reads the completed story frame orally. The class evaluates the finished product to determine whether it adequately reflects the events in the selection and whether it requires additional revision stylistically.

2. **Guided Practice.** The purpose of this stage is to determine whether students have mastered the concept.

    Teacher Action. Guide students to practice their writing and share their experience with peers. Assign a selection (preferably from textbooks) to be read either silently or orally (at a low volume.).

    Student Action. Working in pairs or small groups, students produce one common frame (see Figure 4).

3. **Independent Application.** Students complete frames independently demonstrating their understanding of the process.

    Teacher Action. Make available various frames. See Figure 5 for a sample character frame.

    Student Action. Students can read selections (either assigned or self-selected) and fill-in the appropriate frame. Once students complete the frames, they have a partner edit them before turning them in for credit.

Figure 4. *Sample Lesson. The Plot*

SAMPLE LESSON: LITERATURE
Important Idea or Plot
(Frame from Fowler, 1982)

In this story the problem starts when Paul heard the sound of footsteps while "housesitting" in Mrs. Harland's old, creaky home. After that, he saw something at the end of the hallway that was tall and white. Next, he became even more frightened when he found a note warning him to "Leave this house." The problem is finally solved when the police called saying they just found three young thieves leaving the basement window of the house. The story ends with Paul lying in bed and laughing to himself as he suddenly hears the sound of footsteps once again.

Figure 5. *Character Analysis Frame*

CHARACTER ANALYSIS
(Nichols, 1980)

In the story _by _____

the major character is _who is _____

Another main character is _The problem which the major character faces is

that _____

The story ends with_____

The lesson I learned from reading this story was that _____

_____

Paragraph Frames

Description. Students fill in the missing words in a paragraph about informational texts in a content area.

Goal. Provide structure and format in content areas to help students organize their thoughts on a given topic and learn how to transition between ideas or steps in a process. The frames provide the structure words (such as *next, finally, then*) which aid in the transition from one idea to another.

Benefits. By completing the framework, students develop a logical and coherent piece of writing (see Figure 6).

Figure 6. *Time Order Frame*

ESSAY: TIME ORDER
(Nichols, 1980)

At the end of _what happened was that _____

_____

Previous to this_____

_____

Before this _____

_____

The entire chain of events had begun for a number of reasons including

_____

Some prominent incidents which helped to trigger the conflict were ____

_____

Summary Frame

Description. A summary frame is organized by a series of questions to guide students' thinking while they record important information in content area classrooms.

Goal. Students practice concept/definition, comparison/contrast, problem/ solution, and cause and effect skills while writing to support a claim.

Teacher Actions. Include questions that will result in students organizing their writing to support a claim with these elements.

- Evidence. Information that leads to a claim

- Claim. The assertion that something is true—the claim that is the focal point of the argument

- Support. Examples or explanations for the claim

- Qualifier. A restriction on the claim or evidence for the claim

Student Actions.

- What information is presented that leads to the claim?

- What is the basic statement or claim that is the focus of the information?

- What examples, facts, or other evidence are presented?

- What concessions are made about this claim?

(Northern Nevada Writing Project, 2008)

Wordless Picture Books

Description. Working alone or in pairs, students practice writing using images in wordless books to stimulate creation of narrative that students write, change, and discuss.

Benefits. Students who struggle daily to make sense of the printed word will find wordless picture books less intimidating as a source for writing experiences. Although traditionally thought of as appropriate only for elementary students, many wordless picture books have appeal for students in the upper grades as well. They engage students' creativity; allow for differentiation; use Tier 1, 2, or 3 words (Beck, McKeown & Kucan, 2013); and foster fluency.

Teacher Actions. Introduce students to a variety of wordless picture books and walk them through a book as you project it on the interactive white board. Assign students to groups for creating dialogue and captions for the pages.

Student Actions. Starting with the first page, students tell in sentence form what they think should be written on that page and the teacher records their sentences underneath the picture on the board. After completing the last page, students read the complete book. This may be done chorally, in pairs, or individually depending on the needs of the students.

This book can be duplicated for each group member and used repeatedly to foster fluency and to provide additional practice with Tier 1, 2, or 3 words.

For example, David Wiesner's (1991) *Tuesday,* a Caldecott winner, is an imaginative tale told in pictures where frogs soar through the evening skies on lily pads and invade a sleeping town. Imagine integrating this book with science lessons on gravity, aerodynamics, or on the natural habitats of frogs.

Students view the pictures to interpret the author's purpose and then write their thoughts. For example, before reading the book, possible questions to guide writing are: *What do the pictures suggest to you? What do you think this illustrated story is about? How might you describe in words what the illustrations mean?*

Figure 7 is an example of this strategy in practice that was implemented as an anticipatory activity before a unit of study on gravity. The strategy represents one eighth grade teacher's creative way to spark the students' interest and curiosity and demonstrates the students' responses.

Figure 7. *Excerpt from Responses to the Wordless Picture Book* Tuesday *(Weisner, 1991)*

EXCERPT FROM RESPONSES TO THE WORDLESS PICTURE BOOK TUESDAY
(Weisner, 1991)

1. It is quiet in the swamp and the turtle hears a noise.
2. Leap frogs are flying over the pool.
3. They are flying through the sky every way.
4. The leap frogs fly to a city.
5. A man hears the frogs flying outside his window.

Hoban's (1974) *Circles, Triangles, and Squares* shows how shapes can be found in objects and scenery in our environment. Middle grades math teachers could incorporate this book before beginning a study on geometric figures.

For a suggested list of picture books appealing to adolescents, see Figure 8.

Figure 8. *Suggested Wordless Picture Books for Middle Grades Students*

WORDLESS PICTURE BOOKS

1. *Babe Conquers the World. The Legendary Life of Babe Didrikson Zaharias* by Rich and Sandra Neil Wallace (©2014; grades 5–8)

2. *Fourth Down and Inches. Concussions and Football's Make-or-Break Moment* by Carla Killough McClafferty (©2013; grades 8–12)

3. *"The President Has Been Shot!". The Assassination of John F. Kennedy* by James L. Swanson by (©2013; grades 6–10)

4. *The Nazi Hunters. How a Team of Spies and Survivors Captured the World's Most Notorious Nazi* by Neal Bascomb (©2013; grades 7–12)

5. *Imprisoned. The Betrayal of Japanese Americans during World War II* by Martin W. Sandler (©2013; grades 6–10)

6. *Eruption! Volcanoes and the Science of Saving Lives* by Elizabeth Rusch (©2013; grades 5–8)

7. *Diego Rivera. An Artist for the People* by Susan Goldman Rubin (©2013; grades 6–10)

8. *What the Heart Knows. Chants, Charms, and Blessings* by Joyce Sidman (©2013; grades 7–12)

9. *Lincoln's Grave Robbers* by Steve Sheinkin (©2013; grades 5–8)

10. *Courage Has No Color. The True Story of the Triple Nickles, America's First Black Paratroopers* by Tanya Lee Stone (©2013; grades 5–9)

11. *Navigating Early* by Clare Vanderpool (Math; ©2013; grades 5–8)

12. *A Girl Named Digit* by Annabelle Monaghan (Math; ©2012; grades 7–9)

13. *Mindblind* by Jennifer Roy (Math; ©2010; grades 6–9)

14. *The Mighty Mars Rovers. The Incredible Adventures of Spirit and Opportunity* by Elizabeth Rusch (science; ©2012; grades 5–8)

15. *Moonbird. A Year on the Wind with the Great Survivor B95* by Phillip Hoose (science; ©2012; grades 7–12)

16. *Bomb. The Race to Build—and Steal—the World's Most Dangerous Weapon* by Steve Sheinkin (science; ©2012; grades 7–10)

17. *Invincible Microbe. Tuberculosis and the Never-Ending Search for a Cure* by Jim Murphy (science;©2012; grades 6–10)

18. *Frozen Secrets . Antarctica Revealed* by Sally M. Walker (history/ science; ©2010; grades 6–9)

19. *Lost & Found* by Shaun Tan (©2011; grades 5–12)

20. *Truce. The Day the Soldiers Stopped Fighting* by Jim Murphy (©2009; grades 5–8)

21. *Who Journeyed on the Mayflower?* By Nicola Barber (history; ©2014; grades 5–8)

Caption Books

Description. The "language experience approach" (Allen, 1976) is a fundamental approach to helping struggling and beginner readers that has been around for decades. It has been successful because it uses the students' own language as a basis for their reading materials. The basic philosophy posits that what students can think about they can talk about, and what they can talk about can be expressed in some form, written or artistic. Caption books are authored solely by the students themselves on a topic of their choosing or one assigned by the teacher.

Benefits. One way to use the language experience approach with struggling or reluctant middle grades writers is through the use of caption books.

Student Actions. After choosing a topic that correlates to the subject under study, the student either draws or locates pictures that coordinate to the topic and write captions for each photo.

- One option would be for students to use a repetitive pattern starting each line of the book the same way. For example, "This is a picture of a…" or "Today in class, we learned that…"

- Providing a frame or pattern can also benefit those students who need practice with high frequency words.

Students can use their newly created books as their reading material, taking turns reading them to their partners, reading them independently and expanding the existing sentences with additional descriptive words or other parts of speech.

Double Entry Journal Writing

Description. Another means of helping students write frequently is the double entry journal, dialectic, or dialogue journal as it has been termed through the years (Cox, 1996; Wood & Taylor, 2006; Wood, Taylor, & Stover, 2015). Modifications of this type of journal usually consist of two parts: (a) on the left side, students record interesting parts or facts from the text, field trip, video, demonstration, or lecture, and (b) on the right side, they record their responses and reactions. In some cases, students might work together on brainstorming ideas. This strategy can be adapted for online use through a digital tool such as Google Drive. The students create a four-column chart in their Google document and then provide access to the teacher and other readers/collaborators using the share options. This allows the student to write notes and reflections and give access to another student to read and comment (Wood, Taylor & Stover, 2015).

Teacher Actions. Introduce the concept by modeling and thinking aloud about the processes involved. The teacher and students compose collaboratively with the teacher serving as recorder and thinking and responding to the students. Using an interactive white board allows the class to observe and contribute. Encourage struggling writers to chart their understandings by using pictures with labels or captions. During this portion of the lesson, students can pair up, share what they remember, and discuss various ways of responding to the text.

Student Actions. Students divide their papers with about one-third of the space devoted to the left margin and two-thirds for the remaining right side. On the left side, they will write information from the textbook or other material (or information viewed or listened to). Struggling readers may get their information from pictures in the text in addition to other sources (viewed and heard) to offset the demands of the textbook reading.

In the right-hand column, the students write their reactions. The range of responses could include questions they had, analogies, experiences, surprise reactions, disagreements, creative thoughts, consequences, or applications to other contexts. Encourage struggling writers to chart their understandings by using pictures with labels or captions. During this portion of the lesson, students can pair up, share what they remember, and discuss various ways of responding to the text.

Problem-Solving Writing

Description. The process of writing, which includes planning, composing, and evaluating through recursive actions, is related to the processes involved in resolving problems in mathematics or undertaking investigations in science. These writing activities encourage students to formulate goals and plans necessary to address the task indicated.

Benefits. One area where writing can be used to develop student performance is problem-solving. Various writing approaches can be used to promote the types of thinking and reasoning required in problem-solving situations. The following are some examples of how writing can be used to develop problem-solving methods.

- Designing investigations or describing how to solve a problem

- Comparing and contrasting alternate approaches

- Describing how to use technology in solving a problem

Teacher Actions. Ask students to write in the content areas by organizing their writing to correspond to the specific organizational pattern of the text under study. The most commonly used expository text structure patterns are description, sequence, comparison, cause and effect, and problem/solution. The next section discusses how two of these writing patterns, sequencing and problem/solution, can be used in both mathematics and science to help students organize their thinking and become better problem solvers.

Example 1 Sequencing. The first example is from a sixth grade science class designing an investigation to determine whether soil or water heats faster. Students have just completed working on a physical science lesson exploring heat, temperature, and energy. Through this writing activity, the students are

applying these physical science concepts to earth science
(see Figure 9 for Molly's response to the task).

Figure 9. *Molly's Approach to Scientific Inquiry*

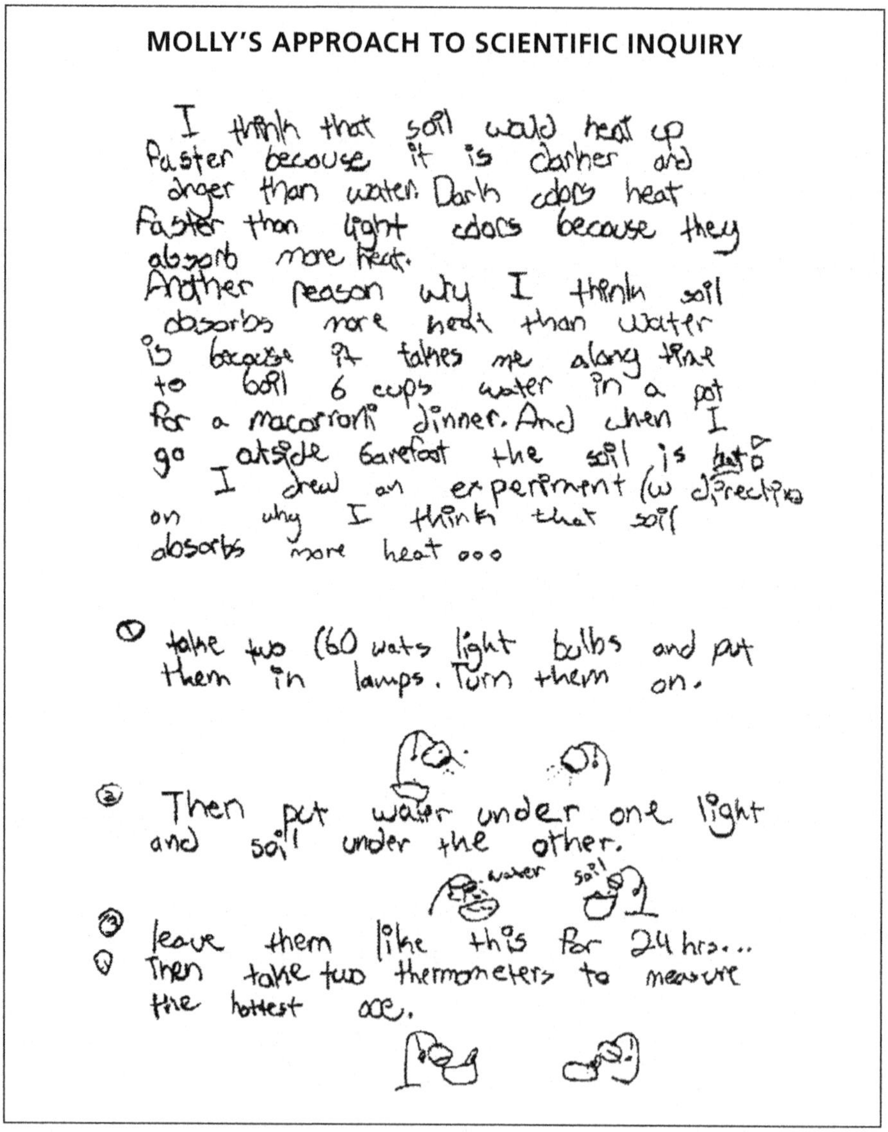

MOLLY'S APPROACH TO SCIENTIFIC INQUIRY

I think that soil would heat up faster because it is darker and dryer than water. Dark colors heat faster than light colors because they absorb more heat.

Another reason why I think soil absorbs more heat than water is because it takes me a long time to boil 6 cups water in a pot for a macaroni dinner. And when I go outside barefoot the soil is hot.

I drew an experiment (w directions on why I think that soil absorbs more heat ooo

① take two (60 wats light bulbs and put them in lamps. Turn them on.

② Then put water under one light and soil under the other.

③ leave them like this for 24 hrs...

④ Then take two thermometers to measure the hottest one.

An analysis of Molly's writing demonstrates that when hypothesizing, she is drawing on past experiences. Because Molly acknowledges that dark colors heat faster than light ones, walking barefoot on the ground in the summer is hot, and it takes water a long time to boil on the stove, she believes that soil will heat faster than water. Molly uses this information in designing her investigation. Molly's experiment calls for using two 60 watt light bulbs as a heat source to investigate whether soil or water heats quicker.

Further analysis shows that writing provided an opportunity for Molly to draw on previous knowledge in contemplating the nature of the scientific question. Additionally, the reflective nature of writing provided structure for Molly in considering the variables in designing an appropriate investigation to test her hypothesis. Molly's writing demonstrates she has applied the steps to scientific inquiry (posing a question, making a prediction, conducting an experiment, and drawing a conclusion) to plan a reasonable approach to solve the problem.

Example 2 Problem/Solution The response of Jamal, an eighth grade student, to a problem-solving activity in mathematics demonstrates a high level of awareness of the restrictions and information given in the problem. His writing provides evidence of monitoring the various steps and processes necessary to arrive at a correct solution. He organizes his data in considering the amounts that he and his cousin will contribute to the family's vacation trip. His self-monitoring leads him to conclude that after the first three weeks that he still would not be contributing $7 more than his cousin. He concludes that he needs to add additional weeks (see Figure 10).

Figure 10. *Jamal's Approach in Solving a Mathematics Problem*

JAMAL'S APPROACH IN SOLVING A MATHEMATICS PROBLEM

You and your cousin are earning money for your family's vacation trip. Your cousin averages $15 a week and receives a one time bonus of $5. You average $10 a week mowing lawns and $8 running errands for neighbors. After working the same number of weeks, you end up with $7 more than your cousin. How many weeks did you work?

I would add $15 and $5. That would give me $20 he earned one week only b/c he only got the bonus one time.

Then for myself I would add $10 + $8 which would give me the total that I get a week. Which would be $18 b/c I also run errands for neighbors.

Cousin		Me		
20 1st week		18 1st week		After adding up the amounts
15 2nd week		18 2nd		← We recieved the 1st 3weeks
15 3rd		18 3rd		I find it is not yet
$50 After 3 week		$54 After 3 week		correct so I must keep Adding up more weeks.
15 4th		18 4th		
$65 After 4 week		$72 After 4 week		After Adding 1 more weeks pay to the 3 week I found that there was $7 difference in our sum of money.

72
-65
7

The way I found the difference in our sums of money was I subtracted the total my cousin had after the 4 week from the total I had after the 4 week. The difference was $7. So after 4 weeks of working, I ended up with $7 more than my cousin b/c despite his $5 bonus I was still making more money. Actually $3 more than him each week, that after the 4th week gave me $7 more than him.

What is noticeable about Jamal's work is not only his justification throughout the process of reaching a conclusion, but his focus at the end in evaluating and summarizing his work. Writing provided a mechanism whereby the student reflected on problem-solving while at the same time giving the teacher a rich view of his thinking.

Problem Solving through Cubing

Description. Cubing (Neeld, 1986) challenges students to examine a problem from six viewpoints that can be modified to meet various situations. Each viewpoint or prompt is written on one face of a cube (see Figure 11). The prompts can be modified to meet the objectives of many learning situations,

Teacher Actions. Demonstrate the cubing strategy to the entire class initially

Student Actions. Generic steps for the cubing strategy are

- Select a topic to introduce or review.

    - Examine it from various sides or viewpoints.

    - Describe it (the process, event, features, traits).

    - Compare it (similar to or different from)

    - Associate it (analogies, makes me think of?)

    - Analyze it (composed of? steps? procedures?).

    - Apply it (how can it be applied to another situation).

- Argue for or against it (support your position).
- Have students informally write their responses.
- Limit the amount of time spent on each prompt.

Students work in small groups to "cube" a topic. Each small group takes one side of the cube and brainstorms their responses while its scribe jots down their thinking on square pieces of poster board. These squares can then be taped together to form a cube. The groups can tum the cube and share their thinking about each side of the problem, issue, or event with the entire class. Turning the cube allows the students to react to various perspectives of the problem situation.

Options. Each small group of students can write about all six sides of the topic (as described in the next lesson), then each group member can take turns writing the group's responses. Together the group members can construct their cube. Another variation is to provide already constructed cubes similar to the one shown in Figure 11 and provide students with post-it notes to jot down their reactions. These notes can then be attached to the corresponding sides.

Figure 11. *Generic Prompts for the Cubing Writing System*

GENERIC PROMPTS FOR THE CUBING WRITING SYSTEM

Compare

Argue

Apply

Associate

Describe

Analyze

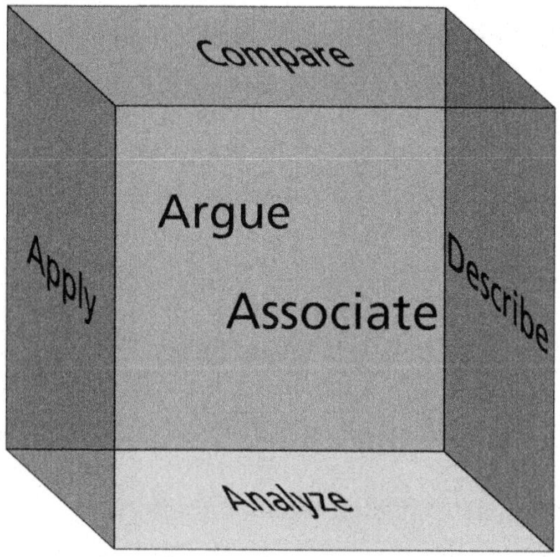

A Sample Cubing Lesson in Science and Mathematics

One approach, modified to facilitate reflection during problem solving, is to have students respond to prompts in a sequential order. Cubing provides a structure for the students to consider various aspects of the investigation and how it relates to various mathematical and scientific concepts.

Student Actions.

Purpose. Explore the process of diffusion using observation, data tables, and graphing skills.

Materials. 3 petri dishes, a potassium permanganate crystal, compass, centimeter graph paper

Procedure.

1. Work in small groups to draw three concentric circles one centimeter apart on the graph paper.

2. In individual petri dishes, place hot water, ice water, and water at room temperature.

3. Each group does a quickwrite outlining their predictions.

4. Carefully place the crystal in each dish and center the concentric circles on the graph paper at the center of each petri dish.

5. Record the approximate radius of the cloud of the dissolved crystal for 30 minutes at two-minute intervals.

Once the data has been collected, use a cubing activity to facilitate discussion of the results. Heterogeneous groups of five or six students brainstorm and write their responses to the prompts. Because there are six sides with questions or viewpoints, each student has the opportunity to serve as scribe. The following prompts might be used to lead students in discovering the properties of diffusion.

- Organize and represent the data you collected.

- Describe the differences you noticed in the results.

- Analyze the reasons for these differences.

- Predict what might happen if the petri dishes were allowed to sit until tomorrow.

- Summarize your observations based on the data you have collected and organized.

- Explore the topic by telling other types of investigations or observations that could be conducted.

Responding to the questions in this order helps students organize the data they have collected and begin exploring relationships and inferences. Groups tape together the sides to form a cube and then each group shares their thinking with the entire class. Have students write a brief synopsis of their finding and inferences to promote critical reflection.

Summary. Writing is a powerful means to help students communicate their thinking and solidify their conceptual understanding. The examples of student writing in mathematics and science illustrate how writing can assist in enhancing the cognitive awareness of students as they engage in learning tasks. Writing supports the development of these metacognitive behaviors by providing teachers with insights into not only what students know but how they think.

Using Wikis, Blogs, Twitter, and other Social Media

Description. There are many digital tools available that provide writing opportunities for students to engage in writing activities online. Voicethread (www.voicethread.com) is a collaborative site that asks students to voice their thinking either orally or in print form similar to a person-to-person exchange of ideas. Twitter, blogging, Instagram, to name a few, are also ways teachers can "smuggle" writing in their subject area instruction while simultaneously appealing to the 21st century learner (Kissel, Wood, Stover, & Heintschel, 2013). In this section, we focus on the wiki, a collaborative writing space where groups of people collectively generate writing and edit the writing of others. Most wiki pages are linked to other pages to show connections among people, places, and things. The connective threads weave together common themes and concepts and offer the reader different opportunities for inquiry.

In classroom settings, students read and discuss texts collaboratively with peers; wiki pages allow them to accomplish this goal via writing. After reading their text and engaging in conversations about it, students add a written layer to the conversation by uploading their discoveries about the book onto a classroom wiki (see Figure 12). At first, each wiki page may contain common information, as shown in Figure 13, including.

- The title and author
- A synopsis of the text
- How characters in the book worked collaboratively
- How characters in the book did not work collaboratively

Figure 12. *Sample of a Classroom Wiki*

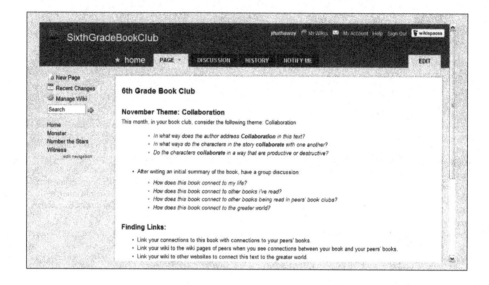

Figure 13. *Synopsis of Book*

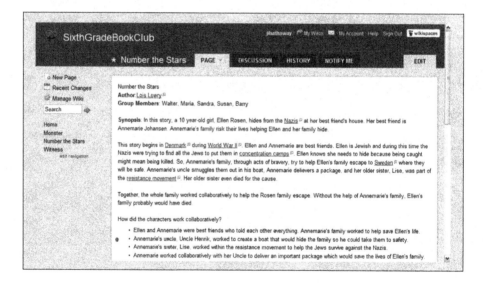

After the different groups upload their common information onto the wiki, students in the class read the wiki sites of their peers (see Figure 14). Together, the group members read the synopses, click the various links to gain an understanding of the broader context, and think about ways their text may connect with the texts of others. Then, the group comes together again to debrief and discuss ways their text connects with other texts. Students may consider the following questions:

- How does our text connect with the texts of other groups?

    - In what ways do characters in other texts work collaboratively like characters in our book?

    - In what ways do the themes of our book connect to our classroom? To our homes? To our community? To the world?

Figure 14. *Making Textual and Wordly Connections*

CONNECTIONS

To other book group texts.

- When we read the notes by the group that read Monster, we noticed that there were teams of people working together to help someone. In our book, a family worked together to save a family. In Monster, a group of people worked together to either convict the main character, or to save the main character from conviction.

To the classroom.

- In order to keep Ellen and her family safe, each character in the book had a specific role to play. Uncle Henrik sailed the boat." Annemarle's mother led the escaping families through the night to Henrik's boat Annemarie had to take the package to Uncle Henrik. If any one of them hadn't done their part, the escaping families wouldn't have made it safely to Sweden. In our book dub, each of us has to do our part for us to be successful. We have to read the books, work together to think about how the characters collaborate, and then think about how our book connects to the books other groups are reading.

To the home.

- In the book there were times when Annemarie's parents could not tell her everything that was going on, but needed her to do what they asked her to do. By not telling her all of the details, they were trying to keep her safe. Sometimes my parents ask me to do things that I don't understand, but maybe they have good reasons for not telling me all of the information and are trying to keep me safe like Annemarie's parents.

To the community.

- The book reminded me that there are groups of people in our own community that are sometimes not trusted or are mistreated just because of their cultural backgrounds. If Annemarle's family was brave enough to help those being mistreated, maybe we should be brave enough to speak out when we see others in our community being treated unfairly. To the world.

To the world.

- This book takes place in Nazi Germany during World War II. Many people think this war took place mostly in Germany, but Jews were being rounded up in other parts of Europe as well, such as Sweden.

To me.

- I didn't realize how many people were affected by Hitler's influence. I always thought it was just in Germany. The Allies needed to do something about the murders.

Through the process of reading the wiki site, reading the links connected to the site, and engaging in conversations about the connectivity of the various texts, students engage in collaborative literacy while they are discovering ways characters in texts work collaboratively.

With the advent of the Common Core State Standards (CCSS), classroom teachers now have a platform from which to provide students with multiple opportunities to interact and collaborate, both face-to-face and in the virtual world (Council of State School Officers, 2010). Wikis are engaging, collaborative, appeal to all learners, and offer virtual spaces for writing. Classroom teachers of all grade levels and content areas will find wikis are easy, free, and rewarding.

Acknowledgements

Pugalee, D. K., DiBiase, W. J., & Wood, K. D. (1999). Writing and the development of problem solving in mathematics and science. *Middle School Journal, 30*(5), 48–52.

Wood, K. D. (1987). Frameworks for teaching the writing process. A strategy to make writing tasks more manageable and usable in all subject areas. *Middle School Journal, 18*(3), 24–26.

Wood, K. D. (1991). Communal writing. *Middle School Journal, 22*(5), 54–58.

Wood, K. D., Nicholson, J., & Griffin, W. (1996). Improving students' reading and writing performance. A matter of life and death. *Middle School Journal, 27*(4), 52–54.

Wood, K. D., & Shea-Bischoff, P. (1997). Helping struggling writers write. *Middle School Journal, 28*(4), 50–53.

Wood, K. D., Stover, K., & Taylor, D.B. (2015). *Smuggling writing across the 6–12 classroom: Standards-based instruction for the 21st learner.* Thousand Oaks, CA: Corwin.

References

Amendum, S. (2015). Principles and practices of effective literacy instruction for ELL's. Keynote address for the University of North Carolina Conference on Literacy, February, Charlotte, NC.

Beck, I.L., McKeown, M.G., & Kucan, L. (2013). *Bringing words to life. Robust vocabulary instruction* (2nd ed.). New York: Guilford press.

Blanton, W. E., Moorman, G. B., & Wood, K. D. (1986). A model of direct instruction applied to the basal skills lesson. *The Reading Teacher, 4,* 299–305.

Common Core State Standards Initiative. (2010). *Common Core State Standards for English language arts & literacy in history/social studies, science, and technical subjects.* Washington, DC. National Governors Association Center for Best Practices and the Council of Chief State School Officers.

Cox, C. (1996). *Teaching language arts. A student and response centered classroom.* Boston: Allyn & Bacon.

Crist, B. (1975). One capsule a week. A painless remedy for vocabulary ills. *Journal of Reading, 19,* 147–149.

Fowler, G. L. (1982). Developing comprehension skills in primary students through the use of story frames. *The Reading Teacher, 36,* 176–179.

Graham, S., & Perin, D. (2007). *Writing next. Effective strategies to improve writing of adolescents in middle and high school.* Washington, DC: Alliance for Excellence in Education.

Kissel, B., Wood, K. D., Stover, K., & Heintschel, K. (2013). Digital discussions. Using web 2.0 tools to communicate, collaborate and create. In K. D. Wood, J. Paratore, B. Kissel, & R. McCormack, (eds) *What's New in Literacy Teaching?* Newark, DE: International Reading Association.

Lyman, F., 1987, Think-Pair-Share. An expanding teaching technique. MAA-CIE *Cooperative News, 1,* p. 1–2.

McGinley, W. J., & Denner, P. R. (1987). Story impressions. A prereading/writing activity. *The Journal of Reading, 31,* 248–253.

Neeld, E. C. (1996). *Writing.* Glenview, IL. Scott Foresman.

Nichols, J. N. (1980). Using paragraph frames to help remedial high school students with written assignments. *Journal of Reading, 24,* 228–231.

Shanahan, T., Shanahan, C. (2008). Teaching disciplinary literacy to adolescents. Rethinking content-area literacy. *Harvard Education Review, 78*(1), 40-59.

Strahan, D., L'Esperance, M., & Van Hoose, J. (2009). *Promoting harmony* (3rd Ed.). Westerville, OH: Association for Middle Level Education.

Wolsey, T. D., Wood, K. D., & Lapp, D. (October, 2014) Conversation, collaboration and the common core. Strategies for learning together. In K .D. Wood, J. Paratore, B. Kissel, & R. McCormack (eds) *What's New in Literacy Teaching?* Newark, DE: International Reading Association.

Wood, K. D. (1986). How to smuggle writing into classrooms. *Middle School Journal, 17*(3), 5–6.

Wood, K. D. (1987). Fostering cooperative learning in middle and secondary level classrooms. *Middle School Journal, 18*(3), 24–26.

Wood, K. D., & Taylor, D. B. (2006). *Literacy strategies across the subject areas.* New York: Allyn & Bacon.

Wood, K. D., Stover, K., & Taylor, D. B. (2015). *Smuggling writing across the 6-12 Classroom. Standards-based instruction for the 21st century learner.* Thousand Oaks, CA: Corwin.

Appendices

Appendix A

CCSS Exemplar Texts for Grades 6–8

Informational Texts. English Language Arts

- Adams, John. "Letter on Thomas Jefferson." Adams on Adams. Edited by Paul M. Zall. Lexington. University Press of Kentucky, 2004.

- Douglass, Frederick. Narrative of the Life of Frederick Douglass an American Slave, Written by Himself. Boston. Anti-Slavery Office, 1845.

- Churchill, Winston. "Blood, Toil, Tears and Sweat. Address to Parliament on May 13th, 1940." Lend Me Your Ears. Great Speeches in History, 3rd Edition. Edited by William Safire. New York. W. W. Norton, 2004.

- Petry, Ann. Harriet Tubman. Conductor on the Underground Railroad. New York. HarperCollins, 1983.

- Steinbeck, John. Travels with Charley. In Search of America. New York. Penguin, 1997. (1962).

- The Great Fire. New York. Scholastic, 1995.

Informational Texts. History/Social Studies

- United States. Preamble and First Amendment to the United States Constitution. 1787

- Lord, Walter. A Night to Remember. New York. Henry Holt, 1955.

- Isaacson, Phillip. A Short Walk through the Pyramids and through the World of Art. New York. Knopf, 1993.

- National Geographic mini-site on the pyramids, which includes diagrams, pictures, and a time line. http.//www.nationalgeographic.com/pyramids/pyramids.html

- Murphy, Jim. The Great Fire. New York. Scholastic, 1995.

- The Great Chicago Fire, an exhibit created by the Chicago Historical Society that includes essays and images. http.//www.chicagohs.org/fire/intro/gcf-index.html

- Greenberg, Jan, and Sandra Jordan. Vincent Van Gogh. Portrait of an Artist. New York. Random House, 2001.

- Partridge, Elizabeth. This Land Was Made for You and Me. The Life and Songs of Woody Guthrie. New York. Viking, 2002.

- Monk, Linda R. Words We Live By. Your Annotated Guide to the Constitution. New York. Hyperion, 2003.

- Freedman, Russell. Freedom Walkers. The Story of the Montgomery Bus Boycott. New York. Holiday House, 2006.

Informational Texts. Science, Mathematics, and Technical Subjects

- Macaulay, David. Cathedral. The Story of Its Construction. Boston. Houghton Mifflin, 1973.

- Mackay, Donald. The Building of Manhattan. New York. Harper & Row, 1987.

- Media Text. http.//legacy.www.nypl.org/branch/manhattan/index2.cfm?Trg=1&d1=865

- Enzensberger, Hans Magnus. The Number Devil. A Mathematical Adventure. Illustrated by Rotraut Susanne Berner. Translated by Michael Henry Heim. New York. Henry Holt, 1998.

- Peterson, Ivars and Nancy Henderson. Math Trek. Adventures in the Math Zone. San Francisco. Jossey-Bass, 2000.

Appendix B

Example Lesson: Reading Road Map for Revolutionary War Unit

In a typical reading road map, the teachers strategically guide students through a variety of texts, including the textbook, as well as additional sources such as websites. The teacher breaks the reading into sections and provides students with a clear reading purpose with suggestions for varying their reading rate. Guides are designed with *location information*—page numbers along with headings or subheadings taken from the text selection—to show students the exact section of the text or visual aid they should read.

Sometimes students have specific paragraph numbers that focus their reading and encourage them to slow down and process a particular excerpt of important content. *Images or signs* provide students with direction about how to read that section of text or related material. Teachers may ask students to slow down to focus on specific content, skim sections to get a broad idea of information, work with another student (as in the image of two people walking in Figure 1, a Revolutionary War unit example), or stop to respond to text through discussion or writing (as noted by the quill pen image). These images support students as they read a variety of texts and show them the importance of reading flexibly— sometimes slowly and sometimes quickly—skimming and scanning depending on the text and purpose for reading. They also serve as visual cues to students about the active nature of reading. The images inserted are usually produced in a word processing program using clip art or images obtained from free or royalty-free websites or other sources. The teacher selects images that match the lesson focus (such as images from the American Revolution.)

Preparing for the Journey. The teacher introduces her students to the Road to the Revolution reading road map by asking them to skim the guide and peruse the related pages in the textbook to see where their reading journey will take them and what kinds of information they will glean along the way.

Figure 1. *Reading Road Map. The Road to the Revolution*

Directions: Welcome to Colonial America where you will navigate the famous ride of Paul Revere in the events leading up to the Revolutionary War.

Pages 212–219 *With a partner, skim the chapter* and share what you know about the events leading up to the Revolutionary War. Pay attention to headings, subheadings, maps, and images.

Page 212 *Carefully read together* the poem by Longfellow at the beginning of the chapter to learn about the role Paul Revere played during this time.

Page 213 With your partner, whisper read about Paul Revere's role in the road to the Revolutionary War and his importance as a historical figure and hero. Use your finger to trace his journey using the map on page 213 in your textbook.

http://mapmaker.education.nationalgeographic.com Determine the number of miles Paul Revere traveled by tracing his route.

Page 213 Compare the map in your textbook representative of Boston in 1775 with the current online map. With your partner, make a "Then and Now" Venn diagram to show how Boston has changed since 1775.

Choose an online source to learn more about these multiple routes. (Be sure to use the website verification form we discussed in class.) Discuss with your partner why we usually hear abou tpaul Revere and not William Dawes or Samuel Prescott. In groups, develop a grid with your findings.

Rewrite the account of Paul Revere's famous midnight ride and include the voices of both Dawes and Prescott.

The teacher gives students an overview of what information and new learning they will encounter, and to maintain interest and motivation, students choose a traveling companion for their journey (or the teacher can assign partners or group members based on ability levels or who works well together).

Teaching a Lesson on Visual Literacy Using the Reading Road Map

Assess Prior Knowledge.

Teacher Actions. The teacher begins the lesson by assessing and activating students' knowledge of the events that led up to the Revolutionary War. Using an interactive white board to display the Social Studies for Kids website (www.socialstudiesforkids.com), the teacher leads students to an interactive timeline of the Revolutionary War and the events leading up to it.

Student Actions. students share what they already know about events listed on the timeline prior to 1775, such as the Stamp Act, the Boston Massacre, and the Boston Tea Party, while the teacher records their responses on chart paper. Anytime information is unfamiliar to students, the teacher builds their background knowledge by showing videos, reading both print and digital texts, and by examining maps and other information to prepare students for new learning.

Teacher Actions. After eliciting students' prior knowledge, the teacher shows students how to use the interactive links on the timeline to learn more about each of the events listed in the timeline. The teacher then points out the timeline for 1775 and explains that students will be reading about the role of Paul Revere's famous ride in the Road to the Revolution.

Gather Your Luggage. Next, the teacher asks students to gather their "luggage," or materials, such as textbook, reading road maps, and pencils before meeting up with their traveling buddies to begin their journeys. In pairs, students skim the chapter in the textbook and share what they know about the events leading up to the Revolutionary War and, specifically, the role of Paul Revere. The teacher points out that the image of a person on horseback in the reading road map cues them to move quickly over the text at this point in their reading and that the partner reading activity was illustrated with a picture of two people walking side by side. Together, the pairs then read the poem "Paul Revere's Ride" by Henry Wadsworth Longfellow to learn more about Paul Revere. The teacher circulates among the student pairs to listen to their conversations, to determine what they know and what kinds of misconceptions they have, and to provide assistance as needed.

Plot Out Your Journey. The student pairs quietly read from their textbooks to learn more about Paul Revere as a historical figure and hero. They use their fingers to trace the route of Revere's famous midnight ride on the map in their textbooks. An image of a lantern in the reading road map reminds them that slowing down could "illuminate" their understanding of the text.

Take a Side Trip. After examining the map in the textbook, students take a detour to the National Geographic interactive map website provided in the reading road map (noted with a picture of a doorway). Using this present-day map, students retrace Paul Revere's famous route and determine the total number of miles he traveled. Next, the student pairs explore alternative routes using today's roads and highways to determine the fastest route possible to warn the patriots in Lexington and Concord of the British advance. Students justify their answers by providing the total number of miles traveled as well as any other factors (e.g., interstate travel, stoplights) that might affect the journey.

Compare, Construct, and Discuss. To continue this comparative discussion, students compare the 1775 map of Revere's ride from the textbook with the online version of a map of the area today and note differences and changes to the area. With the image of the quill pen as their cue, student pairs stop to create a chart to demonstrate how the area of Boston has changed since 1775. In previous lessons, students learned about various types of charts used to visually display information. This lesson allows students to apply that knowledge using new social studies concepts. The teacher's role is to visit with each pair of students and listen to their comments and observations about the maps. To foster deep thinking, the teacher asks questions such as "Is Boston still a peninsula?" and "What happened to the Back Bay area?"

Pair, Share, and Examine. In the next section of the reading road map, marked by the image of a magnifying glass, students have the opportunity to choose how to proceed to find the necessary information for this part of their journey. Here, student pairs choose an online source to learn more about the multiple routes of Dawes and Prescott observed in the online maps. The pairs take a critical stance to discuss reasons that most people are more familiar with Paul Revere and not William Dawes or Samuel Prescott.

Chronicle Your Journey. To allow students to apply their understanding of the information gleaned from the textbook, maps, and online sources, the teacher includes one last stop-and-write along the reading road map journey, again cued by the image of the quill pen. For this last section, students work together to collaboratively rewrite an account of the famous midnight ride from multiple perspectives (e.g., Revere, Dawes, and Prescott). They include important landmarks and geographic features learned by studying the various maps.

Rate Your Trip. The teacher can use these assignments to assess student learning using a self-evaluative rubric that focuses on organization, support, elaboration, style, and conventions. The rewritten account of Paul Revere's famous midnight ride from different perspectives—in addition to the diagrams, charts, and grids that pairs and groups create—provide opportunities for students to illustrate their understanding of the content as well as their use of visual aids.

Benefits. While strategy guides such as the reading road map can take substantial time to develop, they can be used year after year, modified as new information becomes available, and shared with other teachers. In addition, they can be used to emphasize varied facets of reading, such as drawing conclusions, predicting, inferring, critical analysis, vocabulary development, and concept learning. The end goal of any instructional routine is for students to become strategic, independent learners. Strategy guides are one way to foster this independence as students emerge more metacognitively aware of how to gain information from multiple sources of content.

Appendix C

Procedures for Using IEPC (Imagine, Elaborate, Predict, Confirm Strategy)

Modeling IEPC involves explicating, demonstrating, and thoroughly explaining to students what the strategy is and how it can help them learn more effectively. Explaining the purpose of the lesson and the what, the how, and the why, is essential for engaging readers with the text.

Select the Material. Any material with content appropriate for developing imagery can be used with this strategy. This could include trade books, basal selections, newspaper excerpts, or content area or informational text selections.

Display the IEPC Blank Form. Display a blank IEPC form for the class (see Table 1). Tell the students that they are going to engage in a strategy designed to encourage them to use their imaginations to create pictures (in their minds, on paper, on their computersd) of what they see in their minds.

Explain the Benefits. Explain that making pictures or images before, during, and after reading helps them understand and remember what they read and gives them the potential to become better writers by tapping into their creative imaginations.

Explain the Components. Use the transparency, chalkboard, or handout to explain the four phases of IEPC, using language appropriate to students' ability levels. Tell them the first three phases will take place before they read to guide their reading, and the last part, the Confirm phase, will take place after reading.

Table 1. *Sample IEPC Blank Form*

I	E	P	C
Close your eyes and imagine the scene, character,event What do you see, feel,hear, smell? Share your thinking with a partner.	**Elaborate—Tell, describe, or give details of what you "see" in your mind.**	**Use these ideas to make some predictions or guesses about the passages to be read.**	**Read to confirm or change your predictions about the passage.**
Grayish sky Cloudy overhead Air smells Chemical smells Can't see very well I feel choked. Cars, buses, lots of traffic. I am in the city. Factories with smoke coming out of them. There are cars with lots of smoke coming out of the tailpipes	The sky is so hazy, you can't see ten feet in front of you. The sound of horns and traffic are all around. Lots of people are choking and can't get their breath. There's a big industrial park with factories and smoke and chemicals getting into the water. It makes you want to stay inside all the time. The air is so bad, your eyes are burning and red and watery.	I predict some people from the EPA will try to do something to stop it. I think the article will talk about ail of the types of pollution. It will tell about the soot that covers things in cities. And the soot that gets on you from factories. I think it will tell about different types of smog. It will tell how harmful it is to plants and people and animals, too. Something will be done because people's health is in danger. People will have to carpool more. They will have to make it against the law.	The EPA, the Environmental Protection Agency, has changed the old rules. There are two types of pollution they are trying to change. 1) ground level ozone gas is called smog and 2) particulate matter, or soot. Smog is the haze that hangs over cities. Soot is one-seventh the width of a human hair. EPA to end pollution such as carbon monoxide,nitrogen oxides, sulfur dioxide and lead. Bad air can cause lung and breathing problems like asthma. Factories could get fined. Some politicians/ businessmen not happy w/new rules— would cost factories money. Better public transportation carpooling. New rules won't take place until 2004.

Prereading Stage. Often termed the most important stage of the instructional lesson, prereading is when students draw upon prior knowledge, develop background information, set purposes for reading, and develop general interest and enthusiasm for the lesson to follow.

The Imagining Phase. Explain to the students that they are going to read or hear a selection but first they will close their eyes and imagine everything they can about the selection to be read based upon the cover of a book, a title, or a topic. Encourage the students to use sensory experiences by imagining feelings, tastes, smells, sights, and surroundings.

To elicit students' sensory imaginings, use probing questions such as "What do you see on the country road?" "What smells or sounds are around you?" "How do you feel while you are walking there?" "What does this remind you of?" Jot down their responses in the I column of the IEPC form.

The Elaboration Phase. Model how students can use their visual images and add details, anecdotes, prior experiences, sensory information, and so forth that relate to the material to be read.

Talk About Your Thinking. To model elaborative responses, talk about some examples and then ask the students if they have anything to add. Write the responses in the E column on the form.

Use extra textual questions (Hartman & Allison, 1996). Ask questions that require students to connect ideas from beyond the text to information in the selection. "Let me think, what do I already know about where alligators live?" Then use think-aloud responses to provide students with a prototype. "I see a swamp with trees bending over it. It is very quiet except for the chirping of crickets. Only the eyes of the alligator can be seen along the bank."

The Prediction Phase. Talk about at least one sample prediction, based upon prior visual images, and encourage the students to do the same. Write these responses in the P column.

Use the predictions as purposes for reading. Tell the students to think about these predictions as they read or listen to the selection. Explain that, as mentioned previously, they will return to the predictions after the reading.

Reading Stage. Numerous variations are possible during this stage. The reading stage may involve reading a selection to the students, guiding them through the reading, or having them read the selection on their own. Depending on the ability levels of the students and the degree of teacher support needed, students may read in pairs and retell segments to partners or group members or read silently and engage in whole-class discussions.

Have students write down or make mental notes of key information while they are reading to match or refute the original predictions. It may be necessary to model one or more examples of this type of strategic thinking for the class. An example is. "Well, we were right on target with this one, the wolf really did try to scare the farm animals." Another example might be, "I wouldn't have guessed that alligators could stay under water that long."

Postreading Stage. In this stage of the lesson, students discuss and synthesize new information and integrate new knowledge with existing knowledge. It is also the time when students reexamine and analyze purposes for reading and predictions.

The Confirmation Phase. After reading, return to the IEPC form and, using a different color to write, modify the original predictions to coordinate with the newly learned information. Once again, thinking aloud of some sample responses is always helpful here. Write down the students' responses in the C column of the form.

Refer back to the selection. To further enhance understanding, model for the students how to go back to the key parts of the text to confirm or refute the predictions. An example would be, "Yes, that's true because on page 62 it says that volcanoes may appear dormant when they really are active."

Sample IEPC Lesson. Teachers have used the IEPC strategy to encourage students to think and talk about a topic before the actual reading takes place, which also serves to increase their interest and engagement with the lesson. The example in Table 2 illustrates how the IEPC strategy was used to elicit students' prior knowledge and interest in a sixth-grade science lesson on the topic of "Galaxies." Students closed their eyes, imagined they were looking at the sky, and told what they thought, felt, and visualized about the galaxies. Notice how the teacher contributed the elaboration "Light year is the distance light travels in a year" to ensure that concept received the necessary attention. Then the teacher added orally, "You remember we discussed that astronomical units (AU) measure distances between the planets. Scientists use light years to measure distances between galaxies." To further ensure the text-based connection and to introduce some key vocabulary, the teacher contributed the following prediction. "We will learn about a group of galaxies called the Local Group." Then, to encourage students to draw inferences, the teacher asked the class to make some subsequent predictions about this new term. One student response was, "I predict Local Group will be stars that are nearby." Page numbers were written in the C column as an option to illustrate where in the text the correct answers could be found.

Table 2. *Sample IEPC Science Lesson–Galaxies*

I	E	P	C
Stars shining	Light year is the distance light travels in a year. (Teacher)	Predict we will learn that there are more galaxies than we can see.	Galaxies outside the Local Group are moving away from us. That means there are more stars out there than we can see. (p. 376)
There's a dark sky	Looking through a telescope and can see groups of stars.	We will learn about a group of galaxies called the Local Group. (Teacher)	There are 200 billion stars in the Milky Way. (p. 376)
Night time	See the Milky Way.	Predict Local Group will be stars that are nearby	
Groups of stars	There are billions of stars.		
Different shapes			
Billions of stars			
Telescopes			
White dots			

Appendix D

Example Lesson: Ten Important Words Plus

A teacher used the Ten Important Plus strategy to show students how to find and study key words in a text about the circulatory system. First the students were given access to an online text about the circulatory system on the website www.globalclassroom.org/hemo.html. Before students began reading, the teacher modeled the steps of the strategy with a thinkaloud using an excerpt of the online text.

> Today, I am going to teach you how to find and study key words in a text. We are going to read the online text about the circulatory system and use a strategy called Ten Important Words Plus to help us improve our vocabulary and understanding of the circulatory system. First, I am going to read the first paragraph and note key words as I come across them. Each word will be written on a sticky note.

The teacher then read the excerpt from www.globalclassroom.org/hemo.html.

> The circulatory system is the main transportation for the body. The red blood cells act like billions of little UPS trucks carrying all sorts of packages that are needed by all the cells in the body. Instead of UPS, I'll call them RBCs. RBCs carry oxygen and nutrients to the cells. Every cell in the body requires oxygen to remain alive. Besides RBCs, there are also white blood cells (WBCs) moving in the circulatory system traffic. White blood cells are the paramedics, police, and street cleaners of the circulatory system. Anytime we have a cold, a cut, or an infection the WBCs go to work.

After reading the excerpt of online text, the teacher demonstrated how he selected key words from the selection. He pointed out that vocabulary can be more precise and sometimes more advanced in informational text. By thinking aloud about the words he selected and why he chose them, he provided students with an explicit example of how to purposely choose important words. For instance, he selected the term *circulatory system* and recorded it on a sticky note because, as he pointed out, it must be important because it is the title of the selection. Additionally, he chose the terms red blood cells and white blood cells because they were used multiple times in the paragraph, and they were shown to play a major role in the body's transportation system, part of the main idea of the excerpt.

Next, students read the remainder of the online text, selected ten words they thought most important to the selection, and recorded each word on a sticky note. After students finished reading and recording their key words, they posted their words on a class bar graph, with common words to be compiled in the same column. The teacher then engaged students in a discussion about the patterns of their choices and how frequently specific words occurred. He asked, "What patterns do you notice?" "Which words were chosen the most?" "Which words were chosen least?" "Why do you think those words were chosen?" One student responded that he noticed a lot of people chose the word *arteries*. When asked why he thought so many people selected that word, he replied, *"Arteries* is an important word because they carry the blood and without them the circulatory system couldn't function."

The class discussed the selected words and their significance to the online text. Then, using the three key words that he had noted from the first paragraph, the teacher led the class in writing a one-sentence summary of the first paragraph as an example. Together, the class wrote. "Red blood cells and white blood cells carry important nutrients and oxygen throughout the circulatory system." Next, using the words from the graph, the students wrote a one-sentence summary of the entire passage.

Sifting through and pairing down all of the information presented in the text forced students to interact with key vocabulary, examine how words connect to the text, and synthesize the information to get the big idea. After students experienced the words in meaningful contexts and participated in rich conversations with their peers, they moved to the final stage of the strategy. The extension or "Plus" aspect of the Ten Important Words Plus technique engages students in a deeper analysis and interaction with the words. Working in small groups, students were given color-coded task cards with prompts to examine the vocabulary on the bar graph in more depth and to promote deeper word learning. Tasks such as these required students to find synonyms, identify antonyms, and generate sentences using the words, or list different forms of the word such as cardiac, cardiology, cardiologist, and pericardium.

Appendix E

Example Lesson: Integrated Literacy Circles—Cause and Effect

The integrated literacy circles approach involves seven phases of instruction: exploration, explication, translation, modeling, guided practice, application, and closure (Blanton, Pilonieta, & Wood, 2007; Blanton, Moorman, & Wood, 1986). These phases are defined and illustrated below in the following lesson taught by one middle school teacher. The students were learning about cause and effect during a unit on desertification in social studies class.

Exploration Phase: During the exploration phase, the teacher elicits and probes students' prior knowledge about the reading task to be performed.

The purpose of the lesson today is to learn about another important text feature called "cause and effect." Cause and effect is one way an author organizes the writing to present the information in an orderly way. It is often used to teach social studies and science concepts. Who can tell me what they think cause and effect means? Why would it be important to understand this relationship?

Explication Phase: During the explication phase, the teacher explains (1) what the task is, (2) the procedures for the task and what knowledge is needed, and (3) when the knowledge can be applied and why. During this phase, the students begin to become aware of the strategies and tasks needed to become better readers.

(1) What the task is
The teacher begins by introducing the concept of cause and effect in terms the students could understand. *Cause and effect is the relationship between two things when one thing makes something else happen. For example, if it*

is raining outside, we use an umbrella. Raining is the "cause"; using an umbrella is the "effect". Writers use this structure to show order, inform, speculate, and change behavior. Whether you realize it or not, you use cause and effect every day to solve problems and make decisions.

(2) Procedures for the task

Next, the teacher outlines the basic procedure for recognizing cause and effect relationships and provides a handout explaining four strategies for identifying cause and effect:

1. Look for stated cause and effect relationships.
2. Look for unstated cause and effect relationships.
3. Look for signal words.
4. Look for effects that are also causes.

The teacher also teaches students how to use the information on the handout and gives them an opportunity to practice. *For today, the first thing you need to do is to look at the handout I have given you. While you're reading, see if you can identify cause and effect relationships. If it is a stated cause and effect, it will probably be easier to find. If it is unstated, it may be a bit more difficult. Look for signal words (because, so, so that, if … then, consequently, as a result) that you can use to help you identify these relationships. It might be helpful to circle the signal words while you locate the causes and effects, or you could put a C over the cause and an E over the effect. This may help you keep the relationship between ideas clear.*

(3) When the knowledge can be applied and why

Finally, the teacher provides conditional knowledge, explaining when and why they would analyze the cause and effect structure of a text. *The cause and effect structure of text gives reasons and explanations for events, conditions, or behavior. Looking for the reason why things happen, such as cause and effect, is a basic human compulsion. So, understanding the cause and effect text structure is essential in learning the basic ways the world works. Knowing this text structure will help you understand important concepts in social studies and science.*

Translation Phase: As the name implies, the teacher asks students to translate or explain the task in their own words. In this way, the teacher can judge how well students are interpreting and understanding the language needed for comprehending the task. For example: *Using your own words, who can tell me what a cause and effect relationship is? Why would knowing this text structure be important and helpful to you? Who can give me an example?*

Modeling Phase: During this stage, the teacher models and demonstrates by thinking aloud how the knowledge is coordinated to complete the task. This process makes implicit thinking processes explicit. For example: *For practice, let's try it! I have written some examples on the board of cause and effect, showing the relationship between two things when one thing makes the other thing happen. If I can put two things into a sentence using "if … then …," I have the requirements for cause and effect. Here are some examples I have written.*

Save money ☞ travel abroad
Eat too much ☞ gain weight
Study politics ☞ become a lawyer
Stay out in the sun too long ☞ get a burn

As you can see, I am able to insert "If … then"; therefore, I have met the requirements for cause and effect. Now, look again at the handout I have given you on desertification. Follow as I read aloud from the overhead projector and note how I locate the causes and effects. It might be helpful to write C above the cause and an E above the effect. Or, you might want to use your markers and color-code the cause and effect in each example. But you may copy what I do.

Guided Practice Phase: After feeling comfortable that the students understand the integrative task that relates to the content under study, the teacher assigns students to work with partners or small groups to coordinate and enact the knowledge to accomplish the reading task. Each student's verbalizing of the thinking processes affects the thinking processes of the group, making learning evident to the teacher/observer. Students continue to work in pairs to practice recognizing cause and effect.

Application Phase: In this phase, the teacher asks students to independently accomplish the task they completed in the previous phases using new, but similar, material. Handouts or web-based activities could be used to help students apply what they had learned.

Closure Phase: To culminate the lesson, the teacher asks the students to summarize what they have learned about performing the target task—both the literacy skill and the content material. With teacher prompts, students discuss the knowledge they used and their understanding of how it was used. Here, they synthesize the contributions of other group and class members and revise their understanding of the task and how they might perform it better next time.

To help students reflect on how the lesson phases helped them understand both the content area concepts and the skills needed to fully comprehend those concepts, teachers can provide a Student Reaction/Reflection Form (see page 36). A reflection form does not need to be completed each time an integrated literacy circle is conducted; however, it is helpful when a new skill is being introduced. Reflecting on the process and on the information learned will highlight key information for students, which, in turn, will help them remember the information more easily.

Appendix F

Example Lesson: Pick a Word—Not Just Any Word

This lesson illustrates how an eighth grade class of students chose vocabulary words as part of a Holocaust unit. Requiring at least five class periods to complete, the Holocaust unit is based on informational texts and Internet sites. Teachers of the unit selected different passages about different aspects of the Holocaust, such as the Nuremburg race laws, Nazi propaganda, and deportation. They chose passages that were of manageable length, well-written, and informative in ways that would capture and maintain student interest. In addition, they chose different passages about the same topic for one phase of the instructional framework.

Another important aspect of the instruction consisted of individual, group, and whole-class formats. First, teachers divided the class into two large groups, giving each group a different topic related to the Holocaust—racism and Nazi propaganda. Then they divided the large groups into two subgroups who read about the same topic but from different sources. For example, each subgroup of the large group assigned the topic of Nazi propaganda read either a passage entitled "Nazi Propaganda" or another passage entitled "Nazi Propaganda and Censorship." To cover other topics related to the Holocaust, teachers conducted two rounds using the same procedure of dividing the class into large groups and then subgroups (see Figure 1).

Figure 1. *Flow Chart for "Pick a Word-Not Just Any Word"*

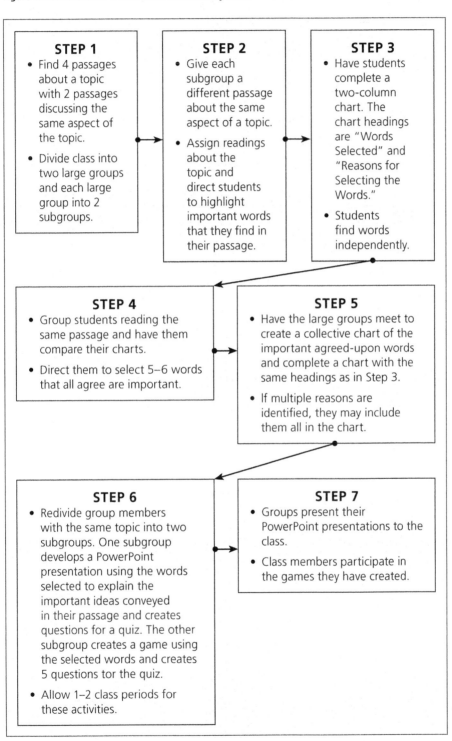

Phase 1. Individual Reading of the Text. After dividing the class into two large groups and then further subdividing each large group into two subgroups, teachers assigned passages to each subgroup. At this point, all students read their assigned passage independently and coded the text by underlining important ideas and circling critical words and phrases. The teacher circulated the room, clarifying confusions and answering student questions. The students then completed a chart (see Figure 2) on which they listed the circled words and provided a reason each word was important for understanding the passage. Figure 2 provides an example from a group that read a passage entitled "Nazi Propaganda and Censorship."

Figure 2. *Worksheet 1*

	Words readers need to know to understand this passage	Why readers need to know these words
	WORD SAMPLE SELECTED BY THE SUBGROUP THAT READ "NAZI PROPAGANDA AND CENSORSHIP"	
John	Adolf Hitler	He was the leader. He made the Jews feel lower than human.
	Nazis	They controlled the camps.
	freedom	The Jews needed freedom.
	Jewish	The Jewish people suffered a lot.
Elliot	democracy	Because there is going to be a great change in government.
	dictatorship	It's the opposite of democracy and this was how Hitler took power.
	loyalty	They needed it for the people to cooperate and unite.

	Words readers need to know to understand this passage	Why readers need to know these words
	WORD SAMPLE SELECTED BY THE SUBGROUP THAT READ "NAZI PROPAGANDA"	
Samuel	propaganda	To understand the main idea of the passage
	anti-Semitism	To understand what they are saying in the passage
	genocide	To know what they did to the Jews
	benevolent	To know what the Nazis wanted people to speak
Darrell	propaganda	So [you] could know what it's talking about in the first two paragraphs
	doctrine	Hitler used it to explain his plan in a book.
	anti-Semitism	I think it has something to do with racism.
	genocide	Nazis were people who did bad things and genocide was one of them.

Phase 2. Same Text Small Subgroups. After reading the passage and completing their lists of important words, the students met with other students who read the same passage. These subgroups compared their lists of words and then decided as a group which words to teach to the class, noting, in particular, which words had been selected by more than one group member. Through discussion and negotiation, they collectively decided which of the five to eight words were the most valuable for understanding the passage and entered them in a chart shown in Figure 3, on which they wrote the words and provided a reason the subgroup considered each to be important.

Figure 3. *Worksheet 2A*

WORD SAMPLE OF SUBGROUP FOR "NAZI PROPAGANDA AND CENSORSHIP"	
Words that group members believe everyone should know	Why everyone should know this word
anti-Semitism	The Nazis had [their] way to teach the children.
tyranny	The Nazis treated the Jews badly with unjust force.
propaganda	The Nazis used this to influence the people.
Jews	They suffered by the hands of the Nazi Party. They used cruel tactics.
WORD SAMPLE OF SUBGROUP FOR "NAZI PROPAGANDA"	
Words that group members believe everyone should know	Why everyone should know this word
propaganda	It's in the title.
anti-Semitism	Hitler treated the Jews with discrimination.
genocide	What Hitler tried to do to the Jews.
benevolent	To know [how] Hitler wanted the Jews to speak.

Addressing the reasons a word is important helps students think more deeply about the concept and, in turn, become more engaged in learning about that concept. Based on their reading of the passage, the subgroup wrote information they thought everyone should know as shown in Figure 4.

Figure 4. *Worksheet 2B*

> ## SAMPLE OF COLLECTIVE INFORMATION PROVIDED BYSUBGROUPS INFORMATION EVERYONE WILL LEARN FROM THIS PASSAGE
>
> **"Nazi Propaganda and Censorship"**
>
> Books were burned from German libraries.
>
> Hitler made Jews feel lower than human.
>
> Nazi propaganda influenced the people.
>
> Censorship was used because they wanted people
>
> to know only what they wanted them to know.
>
> **"Nazi Propaganda"**
>
> Hitler thought pure Germans were the supreme people.
>
> How the Jews were treated at the camps.
>
> That the Jews had to send cards home saying they were fine.
>
> The Jews lived in Ghettos.

Sample of subgroups' collective information that everyone will learn from this passage

Nazi Propaganda and Censorship. Books from German libraries were burned. Hitler made Jews feel lower than human. Nazi propaganda influenced the people.

Censorship was used because they wanted people to know only what they wanted them to know.

Nazi Propaganda. Hitler thought pure Germans were the supreme people. How the Jews were treated at the camps. The Jews had to send cards home saying they were fine. The Jews lived in ghettos.

Phase 3. Same Topic Large Groups. After the subgroups completed their work, the students reading about the same topic met as a large group. Each subgroup selected a spokesperson to share the words and information about its passage. The group then compared the words and information about the topic, noting any important overlaps as well as new information. At this point, the group members had to decide which words and information to include in their teaching presentation. They listed the words, their reasons for selecting the words, and the important information about the topic as shown in Figure 5.

Figure 5. *Worksheet 3*

LARGE-GROUP INFORMATION SHEET	
Words to include in the presentation	Why they are important
propaganda	The Nazis used this to influence the people. They used magazines and music to brainwash Germans.
anti~Semitism	Nazis were against Jews and they were trying to get children to learn that.
atrocities	How the U.s. and other Jews thought about the deaths. They thought they were not right.
Hitler	Main leader of Nazis and inflicted major damage on Jews.
Jews	Suffered from Hitler's torture.
tyranny	Nazis treated Jews horribly.
censorship	Because they burned the books and stuff that had to with Jews.

Source. Harmon, J.M., Wood, K.D., & Hedrick, W.B. (2006). *Instructional strategies for teaching content vocabulary Grades 4–12*. Westerville, OH & Newark, DE. National Middle School Association & International Reading Association.

Phase 4. Teaching-the-class activities. The participants in each large group chose one of two tasks. (a) developing a digital visual presentation or (b) creating a review game. Both groups used Worksheet 3 to create their product.

Assessment. At each phase of work, the teacher continually assessed each student's work as well as each group's progress toward completing the tasks. She monitored their choice of words and nudged them to think more deeply about the importance of the terms they selected. In addition, she developed a checklist that served as a guide for the students and a rubric for evaluating the final student-created products that showcased their knowledge of the vocabulary words.

Figure 6 contains a schematic for the different groups at each phase.

Figure 6. *Group Formats for Steps in Figure 7*

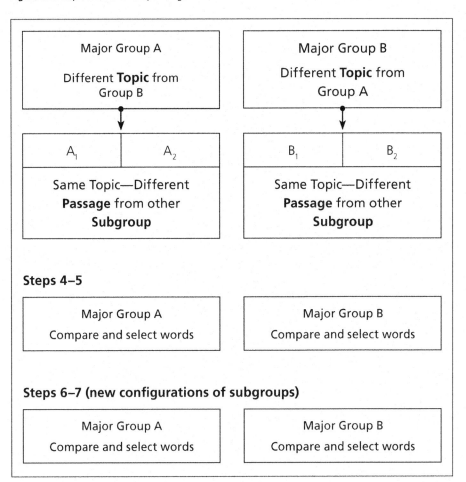

Major Group A

Different **Topic** from Group B

↓

A₁ | A₂

Same Topic—Different **Passage** from other **Subgroup**

Major Group B

Different **Topic** from Group A

↓

B₁ | B₂

Same Topic—Different **Passage** from other **Subgroup**

Steps 4–5

Major Group A
Compare and select words

Major Group B
Compare and select words

Steps 6–7 (new configurations of subgroups)

Major Group A
Compare and select words

Major Group B
Compare and select words

CPSIA information can be obtained at www.ICGtesting.com
Printed in the USA
BVOW09s2055230415

397379BV00002B/3/P

9 781560 902706